Le CID *and* The LIAR

WORKS BY RICHARD WILBUR

Corneille's *Le Cid* and *The Liar*
(translator)

Corneille's *Theatre of Illusion*
(translator)

Collected Poems, 1943–2004

Molière's *Don Juan* (translator)

Mayflies: New Poems and
Translations

The Catbird's Song: Prose
Pieces, 1963–1995

Molière's *Amphitryon* (translator)

Molière's *The School for Husbands*
and *Sganarelle* (translator)

More Opposites

New and Collected Poems

Racine's *Phaedra* (translator)

Racine's *Andromache* (translator)

Loudmouse (for children)

Molière's *The Learned Ladies*
(translator)

The Mind-Reader: New Poems

Responses: Prose Pieces,
1948–1976

Opposites

Molière's *The School for Wives*
(translator)

Walking to Sleep: New Poems
and Translations

Shakespeare: Poems
(coeditor, with Alfred Harbage)

Molière's *Tartuffe* (translator)

The Poems of Richard Wilbur

Advice to a Prophet and Other
Poems

Poe: Complete Poems (editor)

Candide: A Comic Operetta
(with Lillian Hellman)

Poems, 1943–1956

Things of This World

A Bestiary (editor, with Alexander
Calder)

Molière's *The Misanthrope*
(translator)

Ceremony and Other Poems

The Beautiful Changes and
Other Poems

Le CID *and*
The LIAR

Pierre Corneille

Translated and with an Introduction by
RICHARD WILBUR

Mariner Books   Houghton Mifflin Harcourt
BOSTON   NEW YORK   2009

First Mariner Books edition 2009

English translation copyright © 2009 by Richard Wilbur

www.hmhbooks.com

Library of Congress Cataloging-in-Publication Data
Corneille, Pierre, 1606–1684.
  [Cid. English]
  Le Cid ; and, The liar / Pierre Corneille ; translated and with an
introduction by Richard Wilbur.
    p. cm.
  ISBN 978-0-15-603583-5
  1. Cid, ca. 1043–1099—Drama. I. Wilbur, Richard, 1921– II. Corneille,
Pierre, 1606–1684. Menteur. English. III. Title. IV. Title: Liar.
  PQ1749.E5W55 2009
  842'.4—dc22   2008049492

Book design by Melissa Lotfy

Printed in the United States of America

DOC 10 9 8 7 6 5 4 3 2 1

Passages from these translations of *Le Cid* and *The Liar* appeared in *Parnassus, The North Dakota Quarterly, The Yale Review,* and *The Hudson Review.*

For David and Lisa

for David and Lisa

Le CID

1636

Introduction

PIERRE CORNEILLE, a thirty-year-old Rouen lawyer who had written a number of plays, chiefly comedies, was at once a major dramatist when — in late 1636 or early 1637 — *Le Cid* was performed at the Théâtre du Marais in Paris. Though attacked by some on formal or moral grounds, it was greatly praised, and became the rage, and was promptly translated into English and other languages. We are told that *beau comme le Cid* came to be a popular catch phrase for expressing approval of anything. Corneille described his play as tragicomedy, a term that generally implied romance, adventure, variety, and a happy ending; but later he decided that *Le Cid* was a tragedy, and that has led to several centuries of scholarly discussion. What we can be sure of is that it is a heroic play.

The hero and heroine, Rodrigue and Chimène, live in an eleventh-century Seville that is portrayed as a warrior culture just beginning to be focused into monarchy. They are in love and, it initially appears, will soon marry. Their fathers, Don Diègue and the count of Gormas, are powerful knights devoted to personal honor: when the count insults the much-older Don Diègue, it becomes necessary for the latter's son Rodrigue, under the old feudal rules, to avenge him, and that means that he must kill the father of his beloved. Chimène in turn finds it her duty to seek, by one proceeding or another, and in spite of her love, the death of her father's slayer. What gives the young lovers heroic stature is that each, while doing what honor requires, continues to feel for the other a love composed of fervor and high esteem. Looking back on his play in an examen of 1660, Corneille describes his principals in just those terms: "Rodrigue performs his duty without giving up any of his passion; Chimène does the same in her turn . . ." In the play proper, Corneille is at pains to state and restate the dimensions of heroic character as he conceived them; prior to their duel, the count expresses in these terms his respect for his young adversary:

> I know your passionate feelings, and admire
> The way that duty regulates their fire:
> Restraint does not unman your ardent soul,
> But shows in you a noble self-control.

Thus abstractly defined, the *générosité* of Corneille's heroes, their greatness of spirit, can seem neat and unshakable. But under the atrocious pressures that obtain in *Le Cid*, its heroes must struggle throughout to be themselves, and that is where the drama lies. In the stanzaic soliloquy of Act One, Scene Six, Rodrigue makes a tormented decision to do his duty, and the infanta's self-conquering soliloquy in Act Five, Scene Two, is a variant of that. Chimène's struggles are the most moving, especially in scenes where she cannot repress her love, then blushes for that weakness and once more demands her lover's head. Both she and Rodrigue are drawn, in their anguishing circumstances, toward the release of death.

The fictional duration of *Le Cid* is but twenty-four hours, and yet one feels quite sure that ampler time will not bring a happy ending. Though in the final scene the king gives Chimène a year in which to dry her tears, after which she is to marry Rodrigue, it seems clear that she will never cease to see her beloved as her father's murderer. In the 1660 examen, once again, Corneille points out that Chimène makes no response to the king's decree; we are to understand her silence as an act of resistance and an expression of her hope that time will produce new obstacles to the marriage. "When kings speak," Corneille tells us, "the only respectful way to contradict them is to be silent."

The Cast of Characters describes Don Fernand as the "first king of Castile." He is not an absolute ruler, but a primus inter pares, and the disobedience of the count in Act One is but one sign of the transitional state of authority in the play. The throne has not yet become the sole shaper of law and justice, the sole center of power. There are voices, beside the king's, which look toward a securer polity, and we hear one of them when the infanta says to Chimène:

> It's noble if, to avenge a father, we're
> Compelled to seek the head of one so dear;
> But it is nobler still if we forsake
> Our private quarrels for the nation's sake.

Unfortunately, Chimène and her lover have been shaped and victimized by the old vendetta system, and though he will go on to military glory there is little hope for their love. As Rodrigue says in Act Three, Scene Four,

> What pain our sires bequeath to you and me!

The diction of *Le Cid* is elevated because the characters are heroic and dwell in a romantic past; because the scene is often a royal court; because there is no comic relief; because Corneille wishes to enforce his moral vision by eloquent formulations;

and—finally—because the level of dialogue must be capable of modulating into the operatic: the stanzaic soliloquies of Rodrigue and the infanta are very much like arias, and the great scene between Rodrigue and Chimène (Act Three, Scene Four) concludes by evoking a duet.

The stylistic altitude of this play is such that Chimène can apostrophize her own eyes and go on to sum up her affliction in a powerful figure. I quote her two lines in my approximate translation:

> Weep, weep, my blinded eyes, for half my heart
> Is in the tomb, slain by its other part!

Those lines are lofty, but they are also full of passion, vigor, and invention. The word that comes up again and again, in scholarly appreciations of *Le Cid,* is "exuberance," and I hope that this translation, which aims at a maximum fidelity, has also been infected with that.

R. W.
Cummington, 2008

Le CID

1636

Cast of Characters

DON FERNAND, first king of Castile

DOÑA URRAQUE, infanta of Castile

DON DIÈGUE, father of Don Rodrigue

DON GOMES, count de Gormas, father of Chimène

DON RODRIGUE, in love with Chimène; her beloved

DON SANCHE, in love with Chimène

DON ARIAS ⎫
⎬ Castilian nobles
DON ALONSE ⎭

CHIMÈNE, daughter of Don Gomes

LÉONOR, the infanta's lady in waiting

ELVIRE, Chimène's lady in waiting

A PAGE

THE SCENE
Seville

The names of the characters should be pronounced in a more-or-less French manner, as follows:

FERNAND	fair-NAHN
RODRIGUE	raw-DREEG
DIÈGUE	d'YEGG
SANCHE	SAHNSH
CHIMÈNE	she-MEN
LÉONOR	lay-o-NOR
ELVIRE	el-VEER
LE CID	luh SEED

ACT ONE

Scene One

Chimène, Elvire

CHIMÈNE

Have you told me all that Father said, Elvire?
Is there anything you've kept from me, my dear?

ELVIRE

His words enchant me still. Rodrigue, whom you
Adore, is so outstanding in his view
That he will soon, if I can read his mind,
Bid you return your suitor's love in kind.

CHIMÈNE

Now tell me once again what makes you say
That he approves my choice; and tell me, pray,
Once more what joys my future may unfold;
Such happy news can't be too often told.
Yes, say again that soon we shall be free
To show our hearts' devotion openly.

Did you tell him how Don Sanche and Don Rodrigue
Both sought your aid in amorous intrigue?
And did you let him know how, having weighed
Both suitors' qualities, my choice was made?

No, no, I said your cool, collected air
Led neither man to hope or to despair,
And that it was your purpose to await
Your father's orders ere you chose a mate.
Those words delighted him; his face was decked
With smiles to hear that proof of your respect;
And, since you'd have me tell it all anew,
Here's what he said of your two swains and you:
"She knows her duty; both men are worthy of her;
Each one's a noble, true, and valiant lover;
They're young, but in their young eyes one can see
The shining of their forebears' gallantry.
Rodrigue, above all, is the very image
Of knightliness and of the man of courage,
And the old warrior stock from which he came
Is rich in heroes who were born to fame.
His father's valor, matchless in his time,
Did wondrous deeds while he was in his prime,
And we may read his former exploits now
In the deep ridges which engrave his brow.
What the father was, I trust the son may be;
If my daughter loved him, 'twould give joy to me."
He broke off then, and went to take his seat
In the council, which was just about to meet;
But even from those few words, it wasn't hard
To see which lover had his high regard.
The king must choose a tutor for his son

[Le Cid]

Today, and he, your sire's, the favored one;
The choice is not in doubt, the honor's great,
And for it there's no other candidate:
So many are his shining deeds that he
Need have no fear of any rivalry.
And since Rodrigue has asked his father to
Convey to yours his hopes of marrying you,
Be sure that, once this council is adjourned,
You'll soon gain all for which your heart has yearned.

CHIMÈNE

And yet, I know not why, my troubled breast
Mistrusts its happiness, and feels oppressed;
Fate, in a flash, can alter for the worse;
I fear, in this great joy, some great reverse.

ELVIRE

That fear will soon be happily belied.

CHIMÈNE

Well, we shall see what fortune will provide.

Scene Two

The Infanta, Léonor, a Page*

THE INFANTA

Page, go at once and find Chimène, and say
That she is late in coming here today,
And that her friend deplores her tardiness.
(*The page exits.*)

LÉONOR

Madam, each day you feel the same, and press
Your visitor, each day, for tidings of
Her heartbeats, and the progress of her love.

THE INFANTA

I have good reason to; I all but made
Her fall in love, and she indeed obeyed;
Through me, her passion for Rodrigue was born;
Rodrigue, with my help, overcame her scorn;
And, having brought those two together, I've
A friendly hope to see their union thrive.

LÉONOR

Madam, you wish those lovers well, I know,
And yet you say as much in tones of woe.

[Le Cid]

How is it that the blissful love they share
Affects your generous heart with gloom and care?
Why should the kind concern which you profess
Make you unhappy in their happiness?
I've said too much, I fear. I've been too bold.

THE INFANTA

No, no. A grief grows worse when it's untold.
Listen, and hear with what I have contended,
Against what foe my pride has been defended.
Love is a tyrant to whom all are prey:
I love this brave young man I've given away.

LÉONOR

You love him!

THE INFANTA

Place your hand upon my heart,
And notice how it's made to throb and start,
To hear its conqueror's name.

LÉONOR

Forgive me, pray,
My horror at this passion you display.
Can a great princess thus forget her role,
And let a simple knight possess her soul?
Have you forgotten what the king would feel,
And that you stem from sovereigns of Castile?

THE INFANTA

So very mindful of those things am I
That ere I stooped below my rank, I'd die.

I might contend that only merit should,
In noble souls, ignite love's kindling wood,
And in my passion's cause I could produce
A thousand precedents as my excuse;
But I'll not follow them, at pride's expense;
My soul won't yield to the assaults of sense;
I am the daughter of a monarch, and
None but a prince is worthy of my hand.
Seeing what frail defense my heart could make,
I gave away the prize I dared not take.
Chimène became his prisoner, not I;
I lit their fires in hopes that mine would die.
Don't be surprised, then, if you see me wait
In strained impatience for their marriage date.
My peace of mind depends on that, you know.
Love lives on hope; when hope's gone, love will go.
It is a fire that dies unless it's fed,
And howsoever much my heart has bled,
Once my Rodrigue is married to Chimène,
My hope will die, and I'll be whole again.
Meanwhile I bear intolerable pains:
Until Rodrigue is wed, my love remains.
I seek to lose him, and I mourn his loss:
That is my inward sorrow and my cross.
It tortures me that, with incessant sighs,
Love makes me long for what I must despise.
My spirit's torn twixt duty and desire:
My will is adamant, my heart's on fire.
This marriage, which I wish and dread, could not
Bring joy to me, or simplify my lot.
Honor and passion both possess me so,
I'll suffer whether it occurs or no.

LÉONOR

Madame, I've naught to say, save that I share
Your anguish at the troubles you must bear.
I dared reprove you; now I feel your woe;
But since your virtue's roused to fight a foe
Whose charms are magical, and to defeat
A weakness that is powerful and sweet,
You soon will calm the turbulence you feel.
Trust in your courage; trust that time will heal;
Above all, trust in Heaven, which would not wrong
Your virtue by a test too harsh and long.

THE INFANTA

My dearest hope now is to hope no more.

PAGE

By your command, Chimène is at the door.

THE INFANTA

(*To Léonor.*)
Go talk with her a moment in the hall.

LÉONOR

You wish to be alone, then, after all?

THE INFANTA

No, I need but a moment to compose
My face a little, and to hide my woes.
I'll follow you.
(*Alone.*)
Just Heaven, I appeal
For some remission of the pain I feel:

[Act One / Scene Two]

Pray save my honor and my peace of mind.
With others' happiness my own's entwined;
Three persons view this marriage as their goal;
Hasten that day, or give me strength of soul.
Once those two lovers have been joined as one,
My fetters will be loosed, my torments done.
But I delay too long: I'll go again
And ease my pain by talking with Chimène.

Scene Three

The Count, Don Diègue

THE COUNT

So, by the favor of the king you've gained
A rank that I, not you, should have obtained:
The young prince of Castile is your tutee.

DON DIÈGUE

This honor, given to my family,
Shows that the king is just, and will accord
To former services their just reward.

THE COUNT

However great he is, a king may be
As human and as fallible as we.
This choice will lead our courtiers to deem
That *present* service is in low esteem.

DON DIÈGUE

Let us forget this prize you're vexed about;
'Twas given for love as much as worth, no doubt;
But we should not offend our sovereign king
By questioning his will in anything.
To this kind gift, pray add another prize;
Let's join your house and mine by sacred ties:

You've but one daughter, and I've an only son;
That match could make our hearts and houses one:
Accept the son-in-law I offer you.

THE COUNT

Your son should look for nobler maids to woo.
The sudden glory of your new position
Will swell his heart with loftier ambition.
Perform your task, sir: let the prince be schooled
By you in how a province should be ruled,
How he must tame the people with a law
That fills the good with love, the bad with awe.
Add to these virtues those that in the field
Lead generals to endure and not to yield,
To use each martial strategy and sleight,
Spend all the day on horseback, and all night,
Urge on their troops to storm a city wall,
And in victorious fight outshine them all.
Teach him by your example, and make him wise
By doing all those deeds before his eyes.

DON DIÈGUE

If he would learn by my example, he
Need only study my biography.
There, in the great career I have pursued,
He'll learn how nations are to be subdued,
And armies led, and how to storm a town,
And how by brilliant deeds to gain renown.

THE COUNT

A prince can't learn his trade from what he reads;
No, he must be inspired by living deeds,
And how much can your years of valor weigh

[Le Cid]

Compared to what I'd show him in a day?
The valor you once had, I now command;
This arm's the chief protector of our land.
Granada, Aragon both fear my steel;
My name's the rampart that protects Castile.
Without me, we'd be captive underlings
Who'd let our enemies become our kings.
Each day, each hour, adds to my acclaim,
And laurels, heaped on laurels, swell my fame.
The prince could, at my side, go into battle
And, under my protection, test his mettle;
He'd see me conquer, learn to do the same,
And soon be worthy of his noble name;
He'd . . .

DON DIÈGUE

      How well you serve the king, I understand:
I watched you do so under my command.
When age had iced my veins, by Heaven's grace
Your gallant heart was there to take my place.
Let us agree, like reasonable men,
That you are now as great as I was then.
However, in our recent rivalry,
The king has made a choice twixt you and me.

THE COUNT

He should have chosen me; you stole the prize.

DON DIÈGUE

The king's decision was both just and wise.

THE COUNT

The post should go to him who'd fill it best.

[*Act One / Scene Three*]   21

DON DIÈGUE

In some respect, you must have failed the test.

THE COUNT

To win, you used your influence at court.

DON DIÈGUE

My glorious exploits were my sole support.

THE COUNT

The king but honors you because you're old.

DON DIÈGUE

He honors only what is brave and bold.

THE COUNT

Why then, it's this brave arm that he should choose.

DON DIÈGUE

Whoever did not win deserved to lose.

THE COUNT

What! I deserve to lose?

DON DIÈGUE

Yes.

THE COUNT

Well, here's what
Your insolence deserves, old idiot.
(*Gives him a slap.*)

[*Le Cid*]

DON DIÈGUE

(*Drawing his sword.*)
Come, take my life. My family, until now,
Has never worn shame's blush upon its brow.

THE COUNT

What do you aim to do, poor broken reed?

DON DIÈGUE

Oh, God! My strength deserts me in my need!

THE COUNT

Your sword is mine. It's fallen, like your fame.
So poor a trophy I'll not stoop to claim.
Go, bid the young prince to prepare for glory
By taking inspiration from your story:
This chastening of your impudence will lend
A pretty finish to the story's end.

[*Act One / Scene Three*]   23

Scene Four

Don Diègue

DON DIÈGUE

O black despair! O treacherous old age!
Shall my long years thus end in shame and rage?
And shall I, who in battle have grown gray,
See all my laurels wither in a day?
This arm, which all of Spain admires and fears,
This arm, which saved the State so many years,
So often propped the throne of our good king,
Could not, in my defense, do anything.
How cruel it is to see my name destroyed,
The work of all my days a sudden void!
How soon my new distinction turned to gall!
From what a height do all my honors fall!
Must I then let the count annul my fame,
And die without revenge, or live in shame?
Count, be the prince's tutor: no one can
Deserve that post who's a dishonored man.
After your foul assault, it's clear that I,
Though chosen by the king, don't qualify.
And you, my sword, with which I did high deeds,
But which a weak old man no longer needs,

[Le Cid]

Which once was dreaded, yet in this attack
Served but for show and not for fighting back,
Go now, forsake a broken creature, and
Avenge me, wielded by a stronger hand.

Scene Five

Don Diègue, Don Rodrigue

DON DIÈGUE

Are you a man, Rodrigue?

DON RODRIGUE

               If you weren't my sire,
I'd prove it soon enough.

DON DIÈGUE

               I like the fire
Of that reply; it comforts my distress.
You get from me that noble testiness;
My youth is in your anger's sudden flame.
Come, my dear son, and wipe away my shame:
Avenge me, do.

DON RODRIGUE

           For what?

DON DIÈGUE

              An act so low
That to our honor 'twas a mortal blow:
A slap. To kill the swine was what I meant

[Le Cid]

To do, but old age trammeled my intent.
This sword I cannot wield is yours to take,
My son, and to employ for vengeance' sake.
Go, prove yourself against our haughty foe.
To wash away this outrage, blood must flow;
Kill or be killed. And, lest you be misled,
The foe I mention is a man to dread:
I've seen him, all besmeared with gore and dust,
Affright an army with his battle lust.
I've seen him make a hundred squadrons flee;
What's more, not only is he known to be
A dauntless general of fighting men,
But he's . . .

DON RODRIGUE

He's what?

DON DIÈGUE

The father of Chimène.

DON RODRIGUE

The father . . .

DON DIÈGUE

I know you love her; save your breath.
To live in infamy is worse than death.
An insult's greater if the source is dear.
Well then, you understand; your duty's clear;
I'll say no more. Avenge yourself and me,
And prove that you are what my son should be.
Meanwhile, I'll grieve for what the fates have done.
Go, go; take vengeance for us both, my son.

Scene Six

Don Rodrigue

DON RODRIGUE

Pierced to the very heart
By such an unforeseen and mortal thrust,
The poor avenger of a cause that's just,
Compelled by unjust fate to play that part,
I stand here stunned, and with a head hung low
  Yield to the fatal blow.
 How near it was, my heart's desire!
  Oh God, that pain again!
 I must take vengeance for a sire
 Wronged by the father of Chimène!

  How am I torn apart!
My honor's what desire would free me of,
Yet I must take revenge, despite my love.
One voice commands me, one would sway my heart.
Forced to renounce what is most sweet to me
  Or live in infamy,
 I'm pierced by thrust and counterthrust.
  What answer is there, then?
 Can I refuse to fight, or must
 I slay the father of Chimène?

    [Le Cid]

Sire, mistress, honor, love,
Delightful tyranny, austere demand,
My glory tarnished or my passion banned.
What one requires, the other would reprove.
O sword, stern gift to a courageous soul
    That's yet in love's control,
    Keen enemy of my chief delight,
      What is your mission, then?
    To avenge my sire in mortal fight,
    And so be sure to lose Chimène?

    Far better, then, to die.
I'm pledged to her as much as to my sire.
By this revenge, I'd earn her hate and ire,
Yet she'd despise me if I passed it by.
One deed would cause the one I love to mourn,
    The other she would scorn.
    The more I think, the worse my plight.
      Come, most distraught of men,
    Let's die now as her faithful knight,
    And do no wrong to my Chimène.

    What! To die unavenged!
To choose a death so fatal to my name!
To let all Spain remember me with shame,
And leave my house's honor sadly changed!
To give my life for a beloved whose
    Love I am sure to lose!
    Enough: it's time my folly ceased
      And I grew sane again.
    I'll save our honor now, at least,
    Since after all I'll lose Chimène.

Yes, I was wrong indeed.
To serve my sire before my love is right.
Whether I die of grief, or die in fight,
I'll have my forebears' blood with which to bleed.
Now let me haste to vengeance; I upbraid
    Myself that I've delayed,
  And that my will has wavered so.
    I shall take action then
  For my insulted father, though
  His foe's the father of Chimène.

ACT TWO

Scene One

The Count, Don Arias

THE COUNT

Just between us, I took one word a bit
Hotheadedly, and made too much of it.
But nothing can be done now, I'm afraid.

DON ARIAS

Despite your pride, the king must be obeyed.
He's much perturbed, and in his stormy mood
Could greatly punish such an attitude.
What's more, there's no defense that you can plead:
The victim's rank, the violence of the deed
Amount to an offense you can't appease
By light excuses and apologies.

THE COUNT

My life or death is in the king's control.

DON ARIAS

Since your mistake, you've shown too proud a soul.
The king still loves you. You could mollify him.
He's said, "I wish it." Shall you then defy him?

THE COUNT

A little disobedience, sir, will not
Deprive me of the high repute I've got;
However great the crime, my martial deeds
Should gain for it such pardon as it needs.

DON ARIAS

A subject may do wondrous things, and yet
A sovereign king is never in his debt.
Be modest, sir. Whoever labors for
A sovereign does his duty and no more.
This overweening tone could ruin you.

THE COUNT

We'll see if that dire prophecy comes true.

DON ARIAS

You ought to fear a monarch's awesome power.

THE COUNT

A man like me's not ruined in an hour,
Though faced by all the forces of the crown.
Were I to fall, the State would soon come down.

DON ARIAS

You brave the king, whose scepter rules our land?

[*Le Cid*]

THE COUNT

And, but for me, would tumble from his hand!
He wishes me alive at any cost;
If I lost my head, his crown would soon be lost.

DON ARIAS

Be calm, I beg you. Let yourself be guided
By reason, sir.

THE COUNT

The matter is decided.

DON ARIAS

What shall I say, then? What shall I tell the king?

THE COUNT

That I'll not apologize for anything.

DON ARIAS

Kings like to be obeyed, as you'll recall.

THE COUNT

I've given you my answer, sir. That's all.

DON ARIAS

Farewell, then. Would I could save you from this blunder.
For all your laurels, you must fear the thunder.

THE COUNT

I'll wait for it to strike.

[Act Two / Scene One]   33

DON ARIAS

You cannot hide.

THE COUNT

Don Diègue, in that case, will be satisfied.
(*Alone.*)
Not fearing death, I have no fear of threats.
I have a heart that no mischance upsets.
I could survive unhappy and obscure,
But loss of honor I could not endure.

Scene Two

Don Rodrigue, The Count

DON RODRIGUE

A word with you, sir.

THE COUNT

Speak, then.

DON RODRIGUE

Would you say
That you know Don Diègue?

THE COUNT

I would.

DON RODRIGUE

Speak softly, pray.
Do you know that he was matchless in his time,
The soul of valor, honor's paradigm?

THE COUNT

Perhaps he was.

DON RODRIGUE

The fire that you now see
Within my eyes is his.

THE COUNT

What's that to me?

DON RODRIGUE

Four paces hence I'll make that clear to you.

THE COUNT

Presumptuous boy!

DON RODRIGUE

Sir, keep your temper, do.
I'm young, that's true; but well-descended hearts
Don't wait to age before their valor starts.

THE COUNT

You dare to challenge me? A rash demand
From one who's never seen with sword in hand.

DON RODRIGUE

We prodigies are not as other folk,
And the first blow we strike's a masterstroke.

THE COUNT

You know who I am?

DON RODRIGUE

Yes. Others fear your fame,
And shake with fright at mention of your name.
The many laurels on your head portend
For me a bitter and a bloody end.
I dare to challenge a victorious arm,
Yet, high of heart, I shall not come to harm.

[Le Cid]

To avenge a father gives prodigious strength,
And your unbeaten arm may lose at length.

THE COUNT

My eyes have long discovered in your own
The fiery courage that your words have shown;
I've seen in you the spirit of this land,
And wished you to receive my daughter's hand.
I know your passionate feelings, and admire
The way that duty regulates their fire;
Restraint does not unman your ardent soul,
But shows in you a noble self-control.
Yes, wishing for a son-in-law who'd be
A perfect knight, I chose advisedly;
And now, beholding you with grief and ruth,
I prize your valor and lament your youth.
Don't think your maiden thrust will win the day;
Spare me the shame of an unequal fray.
There's little honor in such victory;
Where there's no risk, true glory cannot be.
They'll say that you too easily were slain,
And sorrow at your death is all I'll gain.

DON RODRIGUE

This pity, sir, is more insulting still.
What you've dishonored, do you fear to kill?

THE COUNT

Be gone.

DON RODRIGUE
Let's go, then. Spare me your reply.

THE COUNT

Are you tired of living?

DON RODRIGUE

Are you afraid to die?

THE COUNT

Come, do your duty. One could not admire
A son who outlived the honor of his sire.

Scene Three

The Infanta, Chimène, Léonor

THE INFANTA

Chimène, my dear, don't grieve and suffer so;
Don't let yourself be shattered by this blow.
Calm will return soon, after this little squall;
A passing cloud has dimmed your bliss, that's all,
And you'll lose nothing by a brief delay.

CHIMÈNE

My heart has lost all hope in its dismay.
The sudden storm that shook my calm has made
Me certain of our shipwreck, and afraid
That we shall founder in the port, indeed.
I loved, was loved, our fathers were agreed,
And I was giving you that happy word
Just at the moment when their quarrel occurred—
Which, when the news was brought you, made it plain
That all sweet expectations were in vain.
Cursèd ambition, lunacy that rules
In noblest hearts, and turns men into fools!
Honor, which wrests from me my dearest prize,
What shall you cost me now in tears and sighs!

Their quarrel's nothing to be troubled by:
'Twas a moment's flare-up, and as soon will die.
It's made a stir that quickly will be ended.
The king already bids the breach be mended;
And you well know that I, who feel your grief,
Will spare no pains to bring your heart relief.

CHIMÈNE

Such things won't vanish at the king's behest;
A mortal insult cannot be redressed.
Neither to force nor reason will men yield;
Only in semblance can the wound be healed.
The hatred that men's hearts contrive to hide
Grows hotter still for being kept inside.

THE INFANTA

Your sacred tie with Don Rodrigue will be
The solvent of your fathers' enmity,
And you will feel your love the stronger for
Its power to make them harbor hate no more.

CHIMÈNE

I wish for that, yet doubt it can be so.
Don Diègue's too proud; my father's mind I know.
I can't hold back these tears of grief I shed.
I mourn the past; the future's full of dread.

THE INFANTA

Is it a frail old man's revenge you fear?

CHIMÈNE

Rodrigue's courageous.

[*Le Cid*]

THE INFANTA

He's too young, my dear.

CHIMÈNE

Brave men, at any age, are always such.

THE INFANTA

You mustn't fret about Rodrigue too much.
He loves you, and he'll do as you require.
A word from you, and he'll suppress his ire.

CHIMÈNE

How crushed I'd be, if he did not obey!
And if he obeyed me, what would people say?
Would a good son suffer such indignity?
Whether he heeded or resisted me,
I'd either be ashamed of his compliance
Or deeply troubled by his just defiance.

THE INFANTA

Your soul, Chimène, is noble, and in spite
Of your own interest, sees with honest sight.
But, till the quarrel's settled, what if I were
To make your perfect knight my prisoner,
And stand between his courage and his foe?
Would you be happy if I acted so?

CHIMÈNE

Oh, madam! I would then be free of fear.

Scene Four

The Infanta, a Page, Chimène, Léonor

THE INFANTA

Page, go and find Rodrigue, and bring him here.

PAGE

He and the count . . .

CHIMÈNE

Dear God! I'm terrified.

THE INFANTA

Speak on.

PAGE

They left this palace, side by side.

CHIMÈNE

Alone?

PAGE

Alone, and quarreling, I thought.

CHIMÈNE

Now words are vain; by now, they will have fought.
Madam, forgive my haste, but I must go.

[Le Cid]

Scene Five

The Infanta, Léonor

THE INFANTA

Alas, my spirit is tormented so!
I pity her; her lover I adore;
I have no peace; love tortures me once more.
The fate that tears Rodrigue from his Chimène
Revives my spirit and its pains again.
Their coming rift, which I shall grieve to see,
Already gives a secret joy to me.

LÉONOR

What! Can your lofty self-control give place
So quickly to a passion that's so base?

THE INFANTA

Don't call it base, since at the present hour
It rules me with a high, despotic power.
Respect it, since to me it is so dear.
My virtue fights it, but in mad career
My foolish, ill-protected heart pursues
The lover that Chimène's about to lose.

LÉONOR

So then, your high resolve's been cast aside,
And reason shall no longer be your guide?

Alas for reason! There's little it can do
When the heart's addled by some witches' brew!
When a sick woman loves her sickness, she's
Unlikely to respond to remedies!

LÉONOR

Your heart's bewitched, you're happy to be ill,
But this Rodrigue's unworthy of you still.

THE INFANTA

I know that all too well; but learn from me
How love beguiles the heart with fantasy.
What if Rodrigue, I think, should win the fight,
Putting that famous warrior to flight:
I then could love him, after such a coup;
Humbling the count, what else might he not do?
I dare imagine that his least campaign
Would make him master of some part of Spain,
And in a loving vision of my own
I see him seated on Granada's throne,
I see the Moors all tremble and adore him,
The lords of Aragon bow down before him,
And Portugal's as well. His destinies
Carry his fame and power beyond the seas;
In Africa, his laurels bathe in gore.
Yes, all that's glorious in martial lore,
After this victory, will be spoken òf him,
And it will be my glory that I love him.

LÉONOR

Oh, madam, what a great career you base
Upon a duel that may not take place!

[Le Cid]

THE INFANTA

Rodrigue's insulted; the great count did the deed;
The two left side by side; what more do you need?

LÉONOR

Well then, Rodrigue may fight, as you surmise.
But will his fortunes have so great a rise?

THE INFANTA

Bear with me. I'm quite mad. My mind's askew.
You see the state that love has brought me to.
Come to my room and comfort me, my dear,
And do not leave until my thoughts are clear.

Scene Six

Don Fernand, Don Arias, Don Sanche

DON FERNAND

Can the count be so intractable and proud?
Such disobedience cannot be allowed.

DON ARIAS

I told him at great length of your desire.
I did my best, but he'd not hear me, sire.

DON FERNAND

Great heavens! Shall a subject manifest
So little deference to my request?
He shames Don Diègue, and won't obey the throne!
Here in my court, he makes the law his own!
Though as a warrior he may be acclaimed,
I'll show him how such brashness can be tamed.
Though he were Mars himself, there is a way
To deal with people who do not obey.
Despite the arrogance of his offense,
I meant at first to use no violence,
But since he mocks my kindness, you must go
And seize him, whether he resists or no.

[*Le Cid*]

DON SANCHE

A few days' grace might change his state of mind.
Your message came when rage still made him blind.
Sire, when so proud a spirit has been steeled
For war or quarrel, it is slow to yield.
He knows that he's at fault, but he's not one
Who readily can confess the wrong he's done.

DON FERNAND

Be still, Don Sanche. You're hereby notified
That it is criminal to take his side.

DON SANCHE

I shall obey, sire. But allow me, pray,
Two words in his defense.

DON FERNAND

              What's there to say?

DON SANCHE

That for a man who's used to victory, it
Is inconceivable that he submit.
That word is ever shameful in his eyes,
And it's that word alone the count defies.
What's asked of him would make him feel a slave;
He would obey you if he were less brave.
Command his seasoned sword-arm to atone
By conquering the enemies of your throne,
And he will do it for you, sire. Till then,
I'll answer for that most esteemed of men.

DON FERNAND

You lack respect, but I forgive your years,
And the ardent youth that in your speech appears.
A king, who wisely seeks the general good,
Is a better keeper of his subjects' blood.
I tend my people, all their woes I heal,
As the head assures the loyal body's weal.
What you think best, to me's another thing:
You speak as a soldier, I must act as king,
And of whatever mind the count may be,
He'd lose no honor by obeying me.
His deed offends *me*, too: he's shamed the one
Whom I have made the tutor of my son:
Scorning my choice, he strikes at me as well,
And so lays seige to order's citadel.
Enough of that. Ten vessels that display
The flag of our old foes were seen today
Nearing the river mouth, in bold approach.

DON ARIAS

The Moors have learned by now not to encroach.
So often vanquished, they will not come near
This land, since their great vanquisher is here.

DON FERNAND

They'll never view without some jealousy
The rule of Andalusia held by me;
And this fair land, which long was governed by
Themselves, they ever see with envious eye.
Ten years ago, 'twas for that cause alone
I chose Seville for the Castilian throne,
So as to watch them closely, and to take
Quick steps against such moves as they might make.

[*Le Cid*]

As their beaten generals could tell, they've learned
How, through your foresight, victories are earned.
You've naught to fear.

DON FERNAND

                  But naught I should neglect.
Safety requires that I be circumspect,
And you well know that, on a rising tide,
Their ships with ease could reach our riverside.
Yet this report is unconfirmed; to start
A panic terror in the people's heart
Would not be wise, and I shall not affright
Our citizens upon the edge of night.
Double the watch upon our walls instead.
That should suffice us.

Scene Seven

Don Alonse, Don Fernand, Don Sanche

DON ALONSE

      Sire, the count is dead.
Don Diègue has taken vengeance through his son.

DON FERNAND

I feared this outcome when the wrong was done,
And bade the count make peace then with Don Diègue.

DON ALONSE

Chimène is coming here in tears to beg
For justice, sire, and clasp your royal knees.

DON FERNAND

Though in her grief she has my sympathies,
What the count did seems richly to deserve
This just chastisement of his pride and nerve.
And yet, however just his death may be,
I grieve to lose a champion such as he.
After the loyal, long career he led,
And all the blood that for my throne he shed,
Though he was arrogant, his passing yet
Weakens my power and fills me with regret.

        [Le Cid]

Scene Eight

Chimène, Don Diègue, Don Fernand,
Don Sanche, Don Arias, Don Alonse

CHIMÈNE

Justice, Your Majesty!

DON DIÈGUE

Sire, hear us, please!

CHIMÈNE

I throw myself before you.

DON DIÈGUE

I clasp your knees.

CHIMÈNE

I beg for justice.

DON DIÈGUE

Listen to my defense.

CHIMÈNE

Punish a young man's murderous insolence!
He has destroyed the mainstay of your throne.
He's killed my father.

DON DIÈGUE

And avenged his own.

CHIMÈNE

A king must act when faithful blood is spilt.

DON DIÈGUE

In just retaliation there's no guilt.

DON FERNAND

Rise, both of you, and speak with me in turn.
Chimène, I share the grief with which you burn,
And my heart feels the same distress as you.
          (To Don Diègue.)
You shall speak next, sir; wait until she's through.

CHIMÈNE

My father, sire, is dead. His blood I spied
Pouring in gallons from his noble side—
That blood which kept your land's defenses strong,
That blood which won your battles for so long,
That blood which steams with rage, and ill endures
Having been shed for any cause but yours.
War never slew him, but Rodrigue has found
A way to drain his blood on royal ground.
Alas, his body was not far to seek.
I found him dead. Forgive me if I speak
Unclearly, sire, because I'm so distressed.
My pleading tears will better say the rest.

DON FERNAND

Take heart, child; though your loss I can't efface,
The king shall be your father in his place.

CHIMÈNE

You deeply honor me. As I have said
Already, sire, I found him lying dead.
His wound was gaping, and his blood with just
Fury had writ my duty in the dust.
His valor, rather, despite his bitter change,
Spoke from his wound and bade me seek revenge,
Its dead lips using mine to say these things,
And thus petition the most just of kings.
It must not be, sire, that in your domain,
Beneath your eyes, such lawlessness should reign;
That the best and bravest of your subjects be
Waylaid and murdered with impunity;
That some young hothead should usurp their fame,
Bathe in their blood, and mock their honored name.
If this great warrior's not avenged, I feel
That those who serve your throne will lose their zeal.
My father's dead; I beg you, sire, to take
Revenge for me and for your own great sake.
You suffer by the death of one so good;
Avenge it by another's, blood for blood.
Sacrifice not to me but to your crown,
Your noble person, and your just renown,
Sacrifice to the health of all the State
The arrogance that did this deed of hate.

DON FERNAND

Answer, Don Diègue.

DON DIÈGUE

Happy the warrior who,
When his strength fails, can bid his life adieu!
For men whose trade is courage, there awaits

[Act Two / Scene Eight]   53

At the end of their careers, the worst of fates.
I, whose long labors caused our foes to yield,
I, who reaped victory in many a field,
I, who have lived too long, must in retreat
Now suffer insult and accept defeat.
What ambush, fight, or siege had never done,
Nor great Granada's host, nor Aragon,
Nor all your foes, nor those who envied me,
The count did at this court, Your Majesty,
Jealous because you'd chosen me, and proud
Of the upper hand my feeble age allowed.
This head, grown gray in martial argument,
This blood that in your cause was freely spent,
This arm, which frightened foemen would not brave,
Would have gone down dishonored to the grave,
Had I not had a son in everything
Worthy of me, his country, and his king.
He rescued me; he killed the count, and I
Am cleansed of shame, and can with honor die.
If to show courage, sire, and to resent
A mortal insult calls for punishment,
Let it be me alone whose blood is spilt;
When the arm does wrong, the head must bear the guilt.
If what's occurred be criminal, then I'm
The head, and he the arm, and mine's the crime.
If Chimène would blame this death upon my son,
He only did what I could not have done.
Sacrifice, then, this head, which time will bury,
But keep the arm, to lead your military.
Pour out my blood, sire, to appease Chimène;
I shan't resist, but shall be happy then;
Not questioning the penalty you set,
I'll die without dishonor or regret.

[Le Cid]

DON FERNAND

This is a weighty matter, and it must
Be brought before my council and discussed.
Don Sanche, Chimène must leave us. Pray escort
Her home. Don Diègue's a prisoner in my court.
Send for his son. I'll think on this tonight.

CHIMÈNE

A murderer, sir, should die. It's only right.

DON FERNAND

Go take some rest, my daughter, and calm your woe.

CHIMÈNE

Resting will only make my sorrows grow.

ACT THREE

Scene One

Elvire, Don Rodrigue

ELVIRE

Rodrigue, unhappy man, why are you here?

DON RODRIGUE

To write a finish to my sad career.

ELVIRE

Where did you get the gross presumption to
Invade a house that mourns because of you?
Was it to brave the count's ghost that you came?
Didn't you kill him?

DON RODRIGUE

Living, he was my shame.
'Twas honor made me challenge him to fight.

ELVIRE

And then take shelter in his house at night?
What killer ever did the like before?

DON RODRIGUE

I've come here to surrender, and no more.
Don't look at me with that astonished eye;
I've caused a death, and now I wish to die.
The judge shall be my darling, my Chimène:
She justly hates me; she'll condemn me, then;
I shall rejoice to hear her sentence, and
Receive a welcome deathblow from her hand.

ELVIRE

You would do better to avoid her sight,
And the wild rage your presence would invite.
Go; don't expose yourself, sir, to the dread
Fury that she would pour upon your head.

DON RODRIGUE

No, this beloved whom I've dared offend
Cannot too angrily demand my end.
I'll spare myself a thousand pangs if I
Can make her furious, and the sooner die.

ELVIRE

Chimène is at the palace, bathed in tears.
She'll be accompanied when she reappears.
I pray you, go, Rodrigue; I'm terrified
Lest, in this house, your presence be espied;

Think how she'd grieve if slander said of her
That she'd received her father's murderer!
Soon she'll be here. She's coming. She's just outside.
For her honor's sake, Rodrigue, I beg you: hide.

[*Le Cid*]

Scene Two

Don Sanche, Chimène, Elvire

DON SANCHE

Your anger's righteous, madam; your tears are just;
It's time your foes lay bleeding in the dust.
I shall not seek by gentle argument
To calm your grief or move you to relent,
But if you'll let me serve you, I can lend you
This arm to chasten those who dared offend you;
Pray let my love avenge your father's fate;
Inspired by you, my powers would be great.

CHIMÈNE

Alas for me!

DON SANCHE

I beg you . . .

CHIMÈNE

The king's agreed
To give me justice; he'd rage at such a deed.

DON SANCHE

Crimes often go unpunished, as you know,
Because the wheels of justice are so slow,

[Act Three / Scene Two]   59

And victims' tears are all it can afford.
No, let a knight avenge you by the sword;
That is the surer method, and it's fast.

CHIMÈNE

'Twould be my last resort, and if at last
I come to that, and you still pity me,
You may take vengeance for my misery.

DON SANCHE

That's the one goal on which my heart is bent,
And in that happy hope I go content.

Scene Three

Chimène, Elvire

CHIMÈNE

At last I am alone, and so can heave
Most bitter sighs, and tell you how I grieve;
I can give way to sorrow, and express
With open heart my bottomless distress.
My father's dead, Elvire, and in his first
Duel, Rodrigue's keen blade has done its worst.
Weep, weep, my blinded eyes, for half my heart
Is in the tomb, slain by its other part!
And after that fell blow I must take pains
To avenge what I have lost on what remains.

ELVIRE

Calm yourself, madam.

CHIMÈNE

        Alas, what magic balm
Can you provide to make my heart be calm?
How can I pacify my grief if I
Can't hate the hand it was occasioned by?
How hope for calmness when, at the same time,
I love a criminal and abhor his crime?

He's killed your sire, yet still you've feeling fòr him!

CHIMÈNE

Elvire, I more than love him; I adore him:
My passion strives against my wrath; I see
My lover's features in my enemy,
And though I feel a daughter's pain and ire,
Rodrigue, within my heart, still fights my sire:
He lunges, parries, slashes, staggers back,
Now strong, now weak, now dauntless in attack,
And in that clash of love and wrath I'm still
Much torn in heart; but not so in my will;
However love may seek to sway my soul,
My sense of honor's ever in control:
Unflinchingly, I do as it ordains.
Rodrigue is dear to me; I share his pains,
My heart would side with him, but I instead
Recall my duty, and that my father's dead.

ELVIRE

You seek his life, then?

CHIMÈNE

What a cruel thought!
And what a cruel indictment I have brought!
I ask his head, although my heart can't stand it;
His death will cause my own, yet I demand it!

ELVIRE

Oh, madam, what a fearful course you've picked;
Need you embrace a fate so grim and strict?

CHIMÈNE

When, almost in my arms, my father dies,
Crying for vengeance, shall I not hear his cries?
And shall my heart, distracted, offer for
His death a few vain teardrops, and no more?
Shall love corrupt my will and make me weak,
Stifling my honor when it ought to speak?

ELVIRE

Believe me, madam, you could be pardoned for
Less vengefulness toward one whom you adore,
Fine lover that he is. Your duty's done;
You've seen the king; his inquiry's begun.
Shake off this violent mood, for mercy's sake.

CHIMÈNE

I crave revenge; my honor is at stake.
Though love may urge forgiveness or a truce,
A noble mind will look for no excuse.

ELVIRE

Yet you can't hate Rodrigue. He's dear to you.

CHIMÈNE

That's so.

ELVIRE

Then, after all, what shall you do?

CHIMÈNE

To save my name and end my sorrows, I
Shall seek his death; then I in turn shall die.

Scene Four

Don Rodrigue, Chimène, Elvire

DON RODRIGUE

Well then, I'm here to save you trouble, and
To honor you by dying at your hand.

CHIMÈNE

What's this? Where are we? What do I see, Elvire?
Rodrigue is in my house! Rodrigue is here!

DON RODRIGUE

Don't spare me, now. Enjoy this bloody tryst,
And take your sweet revenge. I shan't resist.

CHIMÈNE

Alas!

DON RODRIGUE

Now, hear me.

CHIMÈNE

I'm dying.

DON RODRIGUE

Listen, do.

CHIMÈNE

Go, let me die.

DON RODRIGUE

Four words, and I'll be through.
Then you must answer only with this sword.

CHIMÈNE

The dripping blade with which my sire was gored!

DON RODRIGUE

Chimène . . .

CHIMÈNE

No, take that hateful thing away;
I see in it the crime for which you'll pay.

DON RODRIGUE

Then study it to make your hate increase,
And swell your wrath, and hasten my decease.

CHIMÈNE

My own blood stains it.

DON RODRIGUE

Plunge it in mine, and so
You'll wash it clean, and cause that stain to go.

CHIMÈNE

How cruel that in one day a sword should slaughter
A man, and that its sight should kill his daughter!

I cannot bear it; take it away, I said:
You bid me hear you, yet you strike me dead.

I'll do as you ask; but still it's my design
That you should end this wretched life of mine;
For you must not expect that love will lead
Me basely to repent a worthy deed.
Your father's sudden anger soiled the fame
Of my own sire, and covered me with shame.
What a brave man feels about a slap, you know:
Outraged, I sought the author of that blow,
And found him, and avenged my father then—
Which, if I had to, I would do again.
Yet for a while my passion made me be
Upon your side, against my sire and me;
Judge of my love if, after a wrong so great,
I pondered whether to retaliate.
Should I offend you? Should I fail my sire?
Was I myself a prey to sudden ire?
I charged myself with rashness, and no doubt
Your beauty would have swayed me and won out,
Had I not known that you would at no cost
Accept a man whose honor had been lost—
That the portion of your heart which I could claim,
Which loved my valor but would hate my shame,
Were I to serve my love and heed its voice,
Would scorn me as unworthy of your choice.
I say to you once more, though with a sigh,
What I shall say to you until I die:
I've done you harm, as I was forced to do
To mend my honor and to merit you;
But now I've served my father and my pride,

And it is you who must be satisfied.
Come, take my life now; I am yours to kill.
I've done my duty, and I do it still.
Your dead sire bids you punish me, I know;
I stand before you a compliant foe:
Sacrifice to your sire, whose blood I shed,
One whose great honor was to strike him dead.

CHIMÈNE

Though we are foes, Rodrigue, I cannot blame
Your brave refusal of disgrace and shame;
However I may weep now, it is not
To accuse you, but to mourn my bitter lot.
I know what honor, after such a slight,
Demanded of a gallant-hearted knight:
You only did what duty bade you do,
And what my duty is, I've learned from you.
I saw how, for your father's sake, you gained
Revenge, and kept his name and yours unstained:
And I must do the same; I must requite
My father's death, and keep our honor bright.
Alas! My love for you is my dismay:
Had Father perished in some other way,
I would have found your face, in my despair,
The only consolation I could bear;
Your touch, like magic, would have brought relief,
Drying my tears and comforting my grief.
But, having lost him, I must now lose you,
Curbing my love as honor bids me do,
While hateful duty, with its heart of stone,
Drives me to work your ruin and my own.
Regardless of our love, my will endures,
And my resolve, Rodrigue, must equal yours.

[Act Three / Scene Four]   67

Your vengeance made you worthy of me, and I,
To prove I'm worthy of *you*, must see you die.

Then don't delay, since honor is at stake:
It asks my life; my life is yours to take.
Yes, sacrifice me now to that high cause;
It will be sweet to die for honor's laws.
After my crime, slow justice would be wrong;
Your vengeance and my death would take too long.
That death I beg you swiftly to confer.

CHIMÈNE

I'm a plaintiff, not your executioner.
You offer me your life; am *I* to end it?
I should demand your life, and you defend it!
Another hand must do what I'll not do.
I'll prosecute, but I'll not punish you.

DON RODRIGUE

Although our love may make your heart incline
To spare me, your resolve must equal mine,
And to avenge your sire by other hands,
My love, is not what fortitude demands.
My hand alone avenged our family name;
Your hand alone, Chimène, must do the same.

CHIMÈNE

Enough. You took your vengeance all alone,
Yet now you would abet me in my own!
I too require no aid; I'll not divide
My duty with another; I've too much pride.

My honor and my father shall, I swear,
Owe nothing to your love or your despair.

DON RODRIGUE

How stern your honor is! What can I do
So as to gain this final gift from you?
In your father's name, or that of love, pray take
My life for vengeance's or pity's sake.
For your sad lover, 'twould be a better fate
To die thus than to live and bear your hate.

CHIMÈNE

No, I don't hate you.

DON RODRIGUE

You should.

CHIMÈNE

But I cannot.

DON RODRIGUE

This world is full of slander. Had you forgot?
Given my crime, and your continued love,
Think what defamers would accuse you of!
No, make those tongues be still; bid me goodbye,
And save your name by causing me to die.

CHIMÈNE

Sparing your life, I glorify my name.
Yes, let those tongues of calumny proclaim
To Heaven my honor and my grief, and tell
How him I love I prosecute as well.

Go now, and let my sad eyes see no more
One whom I seek to kill, and yet adore.
Leave quietly in the darkness; be advised,
Lest you be seen and I be compromised.
There would be scandal if it should appear
That I had willingly received you here.
Don't risk my good repute, I beg of you.

DON RODRIGUE

I'd die first.

CHIMÈNE

Go, now.

DON RODRIGUE

What do you mean to do?

CHIMÈNE

Although my anger's shaken by desire,
I'll do my best now to avenge my sire;
And though I strive sincerely to prevail,
My dearest hope is that my cause may fail.

DON RODRIGUE

O miracle of love!

CHIMÈNE

O misery!

DON RODRIGUE

What pain our sires bequeath to you and me!

[*Le Cid*]

CHIMÈNE

Rodrigue, who dreamt . . . ?

DON RODRIGUE

Chimène, whoever thought . . . ?

CHIMÈNE

That happiness, so near, would come to naught?

DON RODRIGUE

And that, so near to port, when all seemed fair,
A sudden storm would sink us in despair?

CHIMÈNE

Ah, deadly grief!

DON RODRIGUE

Ah, sorrow keen and sore!

CHIMÈNE

Go now, I beg you; I must hear no more.

DON RODRIGUE

Farewell. I shall drag out my life until
Your sire's avengers close in for the kill.

CHIMÈNE

If that occurs, I swear I shan't draw breath
One minute past the hour of your death.
Farewell; let no one see you as you leave.

[Act Three / Scene Four]

ELVIRE

Madam, when Heaven gives us cause to grieve . . .

CHIMÈNE

Leave me in peace; I've need now of the deep
Silence of night, in which I'll sigh and weep.

Scene Five

Don Diègue

DON DIÈGUE

We never taste a perfect happiness:
Some shadow falls upon our best success;
Some care, affecting every glad event,
Mars the serenity of our content.
Elated though I am, fear makes me freeze;
I glow with joy, yet shiver with unease.
The enemy is dead who shamed me so,
But where my avenger is, I do not know.
Weak though I am, I've sought him up and down
Through all the quarters of this darkling town,
And used what agèd energies remain
In looking for my champion, all in vain.
Often, in this dark night, I've thought to embrace
My son, but clasped a specter in his place;
And my alarmed affection, thus misled,
Has conjured up a hundred grounds for dread.
I find no sign that he has fled from here;
The dead count's friends and followers, I fear,
Are many, and that thought disturbs my reason.
Rodrigue is dead, perhaps, or chained in prison.

Great heavens! Another specter? I'm aghast.
Or do I see my dearest hope at last?
Yes, it's my son; no doubt of it. My prayers
Are answered, and I'm free of fears and cares.

Scene Six

Don Diègue, Don Rodrigue

DON DIÈGUE

Rodrigue! Thank Heaven I've found you, my dear boy!

DON RODRIGUE

Alas!

DON DIÈGUE

Let's have no sighs to mar my joy.
When I've caught my breath, I'll praise you, for you've
   shown
A valor that's the equal of my own.
You've learned your trade, and in your derring-do
A race of heroes lives again in you.
Through me, you stem from that intrepid line;
Your first great sword blow equaled all of mine,
And by your youthful ardor you became
At once the rival of your father's fame.
Prop of my age, fine son of whom I dreamed,
Touch these white hairs whose honor you've redeemed,
And kiss this cheek, the once-insulted place
Whose shame you've had the courage to erase.

DON RODRIGUE

Sir, I could do no less; it was your due
From one who was begot and raised by you;
And I rejoice that he to whom I owe
My life approves my sword's initial blow.
But kindly don't object if I reveal,
Despite your pleasure, what in turn I feel.
Let my despair speak out, which until now
Your joy did not permit me to avow.
I'm happy to have served you, sir, but I
Am desolate at what I've lost thereby;
Avenging you, this arm deprived me of
My heart's desire, and robbed me of her love.
Pray say no more; my happiness is lost.
I've paid my debt to you at cruel cost.

DON DIÈGUE

Come, be exultant in your victory.
I gave you life; you saved my name for me.
I value honor more than the light of day,
And owe you, therefore, more than I could pay.
For brave hearts, though, amours aren't worth a penny.
We've but one honor; mistresses are many.
Love's a diversion; honor is our career.

DON RODRIGUE

What are you saying?

DON DIÈGUE

           What you need to hear.

        [*Le Cid*]

I'm the chief victim of my vengeance, sir,
And now you'd have me break my faith to her!
The craven warrior and the perjured swain
Are equally disgraceful, I maintain.
Don't chide my faithfulness, but let me be
A knight who's guiltless of inconstancy.
My bonds to her are far too strong to sever;
Though I've no hope, I shall be hers forever,
And since I cannot leave nor win Chimène,
I seek my death, and shall be peaceful then.

DON DIÈGUE

It's not yet time to seek your death. Tonight
Your king and country call on you to fight.
The ships we feared have come upriver, and
Intend to sack the town and waste the land.
Floodtide and night will bring the Moorish power
Soundlessly to our shore within an hour.
The court's in disarray; the people's fears
Fill all the town with cries and wailing tears.
Amid that panic, there's one cheerful sign;
I found at home five hundred friends of mine
Who, hearing of the insult done me, came
With one accord to vindicate my name.
You have forestalled them, but their valor would
Be better used in spilling Moorish blood.
Go lead them now, as honor bids you do:
Those noble warriors want no chief but you.
Go meet the ancient foe who's drawing nigh,
And die then nobly, if you want to die.

[*Act Three / Scene Six*]   77

Yes, seize some glorious moment, pay the price,
And win the king's thanks for your sacrifice.
Or better still, return with laureled brow,
Not just as the avenger you are now,
But with achievements so superlative
That the king will pardon, and Chimène forgive.
If you love her still, the one way you can earn
Her heart's by a victorious return.
But I waste time in telling you these things:
I hold you here, when I would give you wings.
Come, follow me, and show the king that you
Can serve him as the late count used to do.

ACT FOUR

Scene One

Chimène, Elvire

CHIMÈNE

It's not a false report? You're sure, Elvire?

ELVIRE

You'd not believe how all the people cheer
The brave young hero whom they idolize,
Praising his wondrous exploits to the skies.
He put the Moors to rout; if their attack
Was sudden, he more swiftly drove them back.
Three hours of battle saw our men repel
The foe, and seize two kings of theirs as well.
Our leader's valor could not be withstood.

CHIMÈNE

And 'twas Rodrigue who showed such hardihood?

ELVIRE

Both of those kings were captured through his pains;
He bested them, and put them both in chains.

CHIMÈNE

Who gave you this extraordinary news?

ELVIRE

The populace, which shouts his name, and views
Him as its cause and object of delight,
Its guardian angel and its perfect knight.

CHIMÈNE

What does the king say of this brave report?

ELVIRE

Rodrigue does not yet dare appear at court;
Don Diègue, however, has rejoiced to bring
His son's two royal captives to the king,
Entreating him to give, with gracious hand,
An audience to the savior of his land.

CHIMÈNE

Rodrigue's not wounded?

ELVIRE

                              Not to my knowledge, no.
How pale you are! You mustn't worry so.

CHIMÈNE

What I must do is keep my rage awake.
Shall I slight my duty, fretting for his sake?
He's praised, he's lauded, and my heart assents!

[*Le Cid*]

My honor falters, and my wrath relents!
Be still, my heart, and don't impede my ire:
Two kings he's captured, but he killed my sire.
These mournful garments, which express my woe,
Are the first results his bravery could show,
And though the world may laud his gallantry,
Here everything bespeaks his crime to me.
You gloomy things that fuel my laments,
Dark veils, dark dress, lugubrious ornaments,
Sad pomp that his first victory requires,
Protect my just resolve from passion's fires;
And, lest my love should gain the upper hand,
Speak to my soul of duty's grave command.
Arm me to face this hero without fear.

ELVIRE

Compose yourself. The princess, madam, is here.

Scene Two

The Infanta, Chimène, Léonor, Elvire

THE INFANTA

I have not come to bring your woes relief;
My sighs shall mingle with your tears of grief.

CHIMÈNE

My lady: none but I should grieve today.
The danger that Rodrigue has driven away,
The public weal that through his sword we keep,
Mean that I only have a right to weep.
He's saved the city; he has served his king,
And I alone have grounds for sorrowing.

THE INFANTA

He has indeed done wondrous things, my dear.

CHIMÈNE

That vexing news has long since reached my ear,
And I am told that he's as famous for
Bad luck in love as for success in war.

Why does it vex you, what the people say?
This young Mars whom they praise was yesterday
Your all in all, your love, and when their voice
Acclaims his valor, they approve your choice.

CHIMÈNE

The people justly praise him, but for me
To hear their praises is an agony.
Those high opinions are for me a cross.
The more his fame, the bitterer my loss.
What pain it is to be enamored of him!
The more I learn his worth, the more I love him:
My duty, nonetheless, is stronger still;
I seek his death with an unshaken will.

THE INFANTA

Your sense of duty, yesterday, was deemed
Heroic, dear, and all at court esteemed
The self-control with which you rose above
All other claims, and sacrificed your love.
But will you hear a faithful friend's advice?

CHIMÈNE

That gracious gift you need not offer twice.

THE INFANTA

What made sense then does not make sense today.
Rodrigue is now our one support and stay,
The people's hope and pride and cynosure,

Castile's great prop, the terror of the Moor.
The king himself supports the public view
That in Rodrigue your father lives anew.
What my opinion is, I'll tell you straight:
Seeking his death, you seek to wreck the State.
Come! To avenge a father, is one free
To yield one's homeland to the enemy?
Have you good reason to afflict us thus?
What have we done that you should punish us?
It's not as if you were obliged to wed
The man whose sword thrust left your father dead.
That's understood. For our sake, dear, deprive
Him of your love, but leave the man alive.

CHIMÈNE

Alas, I cannot do as you advise;
My furious duty will not compromise.
Though I admire this hero, though I love him,
Though king and people are adoring of him,
Though valiant warriors guard him round about,
My cypresses will shade his laurels out.

THE INFANTA

It's noble if, to avenge a father, we're
Compelled to seek the head of one so dear;
But it is nobler still if we forsake
Our private quarrels for the nation's sake.
Take back your heart from him. If you can snuff
That flame of love, 'twill punish him enough.
For your country's good, then, do that noble thing.
Besides, what can you hope for from the king?

[*Le Cid*]

CHIMÈNE

He may refuse me, but my pleas won't cease.

THE INFANTA

My dear Chimène, I leave you now in peace;
Think deeply, and consult your inmost voice.

CHIMÈNE

After my father's death, I have no choice.

Scene Three

*Don Fernand, Don Rodrigue,
Don Diègue, Don Arias, Don Sanche*

DON FERNAND

Brave scion of a family renowned
As bold protectors of their native ground,
A house whose gallant story is well known,
Whose gallantry is matched now by your own:
Your worth is greater than I can repay;
What thanks I'd offer you, your deeds outweigh.
Castile delivered from the savage Moors,
The scepter steadied in my hand by yours,
The enemy defeated long before
I could have roused our citizens for war—
Such exploits leave your king unable to
Imagine any way of thanking you.
But your two captive kings can fill that need.
I heard them both describe you as their Cid:
Since, in their language, *cid*'s the word for "lord,"
I give you that great title as reward.
Henceforward be the Cid; may that name make
Grenada and Toledo cringe and shake,
And may it show to all my subjects here
That I'm your debtor, and that I hold you dear.

[Le Cid]

DON RODRIGUE

Your Majesty, don't make too much, I pray,
Of the small service I performed today.
It makes me blush, sire, that so great a king
Should do me honor for so slight a thing.
I owe to such a monarch, while he reigns,
The air I breathe, the blood that's in my veins,
And if it were my fate to lose them for
His sake, 'twould be my duty and no more.

DON FERNAND

Not all of those who out of duty serve
My throne have shown such valor and such verve;
When courage isn't wed to recklessness,
It can't produce so splendid a success.
Then let yourself be praised; and furnish me
A full account, now, of your victory.

DON RODRIGUE

Sire, when the rumored threat was drawing near
The town, and all the streets were full of fear,
A band of friends at Father's house appealed
To me to lead them, though my head still reeled . . .
Oh, sire, forgive my rashness if I then,
Without your sanction, chose to lead those men.
Danger approached; resistance must be led;
If I went near the court, I'd risk my head;
If I had to die, 'twas better in my view
To perish fighting for Seville and you.

DON FERNAND

Your rash revenge I pardon and dispense;
The State, defended, speaks in your defense.

[*Act Four / Scene Three*]   87

Chimène, hereafter, will accuse in vain;
I'll hear her only to console her pain.
Speak on.

DON RODRIGUE

       Sire, under me those warriors now
Moved forward, stern resolve on every brow.
We were at first five hundred, but before
We reached the port we'd gained three thousand more,
For, seeing us march by, assured and strong,
The most unnerved took heart and came along.
Once there, I sent two thirds of them to hide
In vessels anchored at the harborside;
The rest, their number growing constantly
And full of hot impatience, stay with me
And, for some starlit hours, make no sound
But, speechless, lie in wait upon the ground.
The guards, obeying my command to them,
Hide also, to support my stratagem,
I having dared to claim that it was you
On whose behalf I told them what to do.
At last we see, by the stars' glimmering light,
A rising tide bring thirty sails in sight,
And soon the surges of the sea escort
The vessels of the Moors into our port.
We let them pass. To them, all seems serene;
On wall or pier no soldier's to be seen;
Our utter silence renders them unwise;
They're sure that they shall take us by surprise;
They heave to, drop their anchors, wade to land
And blindly run into the trap we'd planned.
We rise then, and a thousand battle cries
Burst from our lips and echo in the skies.

[Le Cid]

Our comrades in the ships reply, and come
Forth sword in hand; the Moors are stricken dumb;
Half-disembarked, they're seized by deep dismay
And, ere they fight us, feel they've lost the day.
They'd come to pillage; they encountered war.
We rush them in the shallows and on shore,
And ere they can form ranks or strike a blow,
We cause great rivers of their blood to flow.
But soon their princes rally them; they gain
Some courage back; their panic starts to wane;
The shame of being killed without a fight
Restores their weakened spirits and their might.
Now resolute, they draw their scimitars;
Our blood and theirs are sacrificed to Mars;
River and bank and port are soon no more
Than fields of carnage and of mingled gore.
How many feats that history might remark
Went unobserved then in the cloaking dark
Where each, sole witness of the deeds he dared,
Had little sense of how the battle fared!
I moved among our forces as their chief,
Bade some advance, to others gave relief,
Took fresh recruits in hand and urged them on,
And could not guess fate's verdict till the dawn.
Day breaks then, and it's clear we've won the fray;
The Moors look, and their courage drains away;
Seeing new reinforcements at our rear,
Their will to fight gives way to mortal fear.
They fly back to their ships in panic, lift
Hoarse cries to Heaven, cut themselves adrift,
And in their wild departure pay no mind
To the two kings whom they have left behind.
Their fear has overcome their loyalty:

[Act Four / Scene Three]   89

The tide, which brought them, takes them back to sea.
Meanwhile their kings fight on, helped by a few
Brave followers, all badly wounded, who
To their last drop of blood dispute the field;
In vain I call upon those kings to yield,
But, scimitars in hand, they won't comply
Till, seeing now that all their solders lie
Dead at their feet, they ask for our commander.
I say that I am he, and they surrender.
I send the two of them to you at once,
And the battle ends for want of còmbatants.
Thus, happily, we overcame the dire . . .

[Le Cid]

Scene Four

Don Alonse, Don Fernand, Don Diègue,
Don Rodrigue, Don Arias, Don Sanche

DON ALONSE

Chimène has come to plead for justice, sire.

DON FERNAND

She picks a sorry time to interfere.
                    (*To Rodrigue.*)
Go, I won't force her to confront you here.
It seems ungrateful to dismiss you so,
But come, embrace your king before you go.

DON DIÈGUE

Chimène may hound him, but she loves him too.

DON FERNAND

So I have heard. Let's see if that is true.
Look grave and sad.

Scene Five

Don Fernand, Don Diègue, Chimène,
Don Sanche, Don Alonse, Elvire, Don Arias

DON FERNAND

             Chimène, you may now let
You heart rejoice, for your demand's been met.
Rodrigue preserved us — but, the day once gained,
He died then of the wounds he had sustained.
Give thanks to Heaven, by which you're thus avenged.
          (Aside, to Don Diègue.)
Look how the color in her cheek has changed.

DON DIÈGUE

And look, sire, how she swoons, which serves to prove
Before our eyes the power of her love.
A sudden grief has let her secrets out,
And whom she loves you can no longer doubt.

CHIMÈNE

Rodrigue is dead, then?

DON FERNAND

              No, he's living still,
And loves you faithfully, and always will.
Be calm, and cease to grieve about him so.

               [Le Cid]

CHIMÈNE

Sire, one can swoon for joy as well as woe;
Sudden delight may have such consequences;
What floods the soul can overwhelm the senses.

DON FERNAND

Don't ask us to believe such talk, my dear:
The grief you felt, Chimène, was all too clear.

CHIMÈNE

Then, sire, add one great grief to my complaint;
Say, if you like, that sorrow made me faint,
But what most moved me was a righteous wrath
That he'd escaped me by a noble death.
If in his country's cause he met his end,
'Twould rob me of the vengeance I intend.
Justice, in such a case, would not be done;
I seek his death, but not a glorious one.
I'd have the locus of his dying be
No field of honor, but the gallows tree.
He'd die for Father, not the fatherland,
And his withered name would bear a shameful brand.
To die for king and country is no shame;
By such a death one gains a deathless name;
That our defender lives, I am not sorry;
He's saved the State, and he is yet my quarry—
A famous chief whom cheering crowds surround,
Not mourned with flowers but with laurels crowned—
In short, a victim worthy to be made
A sacrifice to my dear father's shade.
Alas! What use is such a fantasy?
Rodrigue, I know, has naught to fear from me.
My tears, ignored, can't hurt my adversary;

All of your kingdom is a sanctuary
Where, under your protection, he is free
To treat me as he treats his enemy,
In whose spilt blood a stifled justice lies
Which for the victor is but one more prize.
Yes, law being dead, like those two kings we are
But followers of his triumphal car.

DON FERNAND

It's a violent speech, my daughter, that you've made.
Justice demands that things be calmly weighed.
Your sire's been slain, but he began the feud.
His slayer must be mercifully viewed.
Ere you denounce the pardon I declare,
Look in your heart: Rodrigue is master there,
And secretly you thank a ruler who
Preserves the lover who is dear to you.

CHIMÈNE

You call him dear! The source of all my woe!
My father's murderer! My hated foe!
To my just pleas you pay so little mind,
You think that to ignore my words is kind!
Since you refuse me justice, sire, permit
Me by recourse to arms to seek for it;
For 'twas by arms that his offense was made,
And by the same his crime should be repaid.
Of all your cavaliers I now demand
His head, and in return I'll give my hand;
Yes, bid them fight, sire, and I pledge to wed
The victor, when I know Rodrigue is dead.
Announce that, pray, by royal proclamation.

[Le Cid]

DON FERNAND

This custom, long established in our nation,
Under the guise of punishing some wrong
Deprives the State of soldiers brave and strong.
Often it is the case that such events
Uphold the guilty, and punish innocence.
Rodrigue must fight no duels. His worth's too great
To be exposed to the caprice of Fate,
And if that fine youth erred at any time,
The Moors, in fleeing, took away his crime.

DON DIÈGUE

What, sire! Will you abolish for his sake
A code that all your knights have scorned to break?
What will your people think, or envy say,
If he is sheltered by your arm that way,
And seems no longer willing to contend
Where men of honor seek a noble end?
Such favor, sire, would tarnish all his fame;
Let him enjoy his triumph without shame.
The count was insolent, and by him was slain:
He proved his bravery; brave he should remain.

DON FERNAND

Since you insist, I shall agree. But for
Each foe he meets there might be hundreds more;
The prize Chimène has offered might well make
All of my knights attack him for her sake.
For him to fight them all would be unjust:
Let him but once confront a rival's thrust.
Now choose your champion, and choose well, Chimène.
After this duel, don't complain again.

DON DIÈGUE

Throw the field open, sire, and don't excuse
Our daunted knights by asking *her* to choose.
After Rodrigue's achievements of this day,
What heart would dare confront him? None, I say.
Given such an adversary, who would make
So valiant or so reckless a mistake?

DON SANCHE

If the field is open, then your search is done.
I'll be the reckless or the valiant one.
This favor, lady, I beg you to permit;
You know that you've already promised it.

DON FERNAND

Do you accept this champion, Chimène?

CHIMÈNE

I gave my promise, sire.

DON FERNAND

Tomorrow, then.

DON DIÈGUE

No, sire, there's no occasion for delay:
A brave man's always ready, come what may.

DON FERNAND

To fight a battle, and then to fight anew?

DON DIÈGUE

He caught his breath, sire, while he talked with you.

DON FERNAND

Give him at least an hour or two of rest.
But lest this set a precedent, and lest
I seem without compunction to agree
To a bloody practice that displeases me,
I shan't be present; nor shall my court be there.
(*He turns to Don Arias.*)
You'll be the only judge of this affair.
Have both observe the code of the cavalier,
And when it's over, bring the victor here.
Whichever wins, the prize will be the same:
I'll lead him to Chimène, and he will claim
As his reward the promise of her hand.

CHIMÈNE

Alas! For me, sire, that's a harsh command!

DON FERNAND

You now protest, but if Rodrigue should win,
Your heart would make you hasten to give in.
Complain no more of such a mild decree.
You'll wed the winner, whoever that may be.

ACT FIVE

Scene One

Chimène, Don Rodrigue

CHIMÈNE

Rodrigue, how dare you? Here, in the light of day!
You'll ruin me! I beg you, do not stay.

DON RODRIGUE

I've come, my lady, because I'm going to die,
And, ere I do, must say a last goodbye.
My heart could not face death unless you knew
My dying was an homage paid to you.

CHIMÈNE

You're going to die!

DON RODRIGUE

        I hasten on the path
Toward where my life will satisfy your wrath.

CHIMÈNE

You're going to die! Does Don Sanche have such power
That he can cause your valiant soul to cower?
What's made you feeble, and him a foe to dread?
Rodrigue must fight, yet feels already dead!
The Moors, and Father, he met with fearless heart;
Don Sanche, however, daunts him from the start!
How strange that now your courage should grow weak!

DON RODRIGUE

It's punishment, not combat, that I seek,
And my devoted spirit will not strive,
Since you desire my death, to stay alive.
My heart's still brave, but I'll do nothing to
Preserve a being that displeases you.
This last night might have seen my death, I own,
Had I been fighting for myself alone;
But in defending king, and folk, and state,
'Twould have been treason to invite that fate.
This life is not so odious to me
That I'd escape from it by treachery.
Now that my fortunes only are at stake,
You ask my head, and it is yours to take.
You choose that someone else shall kill me, rather
Than your own hand take vengeance for your father:
I'll not deflect his blows, out of a due
Respect for any man who fights for you:
Since they uphold your honor, 'twill be from
The one I cherish that those blows will come;
I'll bare my breast to them, and gladly see
Your hand behind the hand that pierces me.

CHIMÈNE

If my sad duty, which drives me to pursue
Against my will this punishment for you,
Compels you, out of love's intransigence,
To offer to my champion no defense,
Reflect that, in this course you blindly choose,
Not only life but fame is what you'll lose,
For though in life Rodrigue's renown is bright,
Once he is dead, they'll say he lost the fight.
Your honor is more dear to you than I,
Since for its sake my father had to die,
And you, despite the passion you have shown,
Give up sweet hopes of making me your own.
Yet now your sense of honor is so slack
That you can be assailed and not fight back.
What whim has swept your fortitude away?
Why had you valor once, but not today?
Are you brave only when you do me ill?
For other uses, have you lost your will?
And shall you shame my father, whom you slew,
By letting his inferior conquer you?
Come, do not seek your death; that's mine to claim;
And though you're tired of life, defend your fame.

DON RODRIGUE

After the count's death and the Moors' defeat,
What further test of valor need I meet?
My life's a thing that I can scorn to save:
Men know that I have always proven brave,
And can't be bested; that beneath the skies
It is my honor that I chiefly prize.

[Le Cid]

No, in this coming duel, say what you will,
Rodrigue can perish and be honored still;
No one will dare impeach his courage, or
Contend that he had met his conqueror.
They will but say, "He loved Chimène, and could
Not bear her hatred, which he understood;
He yielded to the bitter fate that led
His cherished mistress to demand his head;
She asked his death, which he resolved to give,
Feeling that it would be a crime to live.
He kept his honor; for that, his love was lost;
He avenged his lady at his own life's cost—
By those two choices sacrificing then
Chimène to honor, and life to his Chimène."
Thus you can see that dying in this fight
Won't dim my fame but render it more bright,
And that my willing death will honor you,
Making amends as nothing else could do.

CHIMÈNE

Since neither honor nor the precious breath
Of life can keep you from this rush toward death,
If ever, dear, I loved you, hear my plea:
Defend yourself, lest Don Sanche marry me.
Fight to protect me from the wretched fate
Of being claimed by someone whom I hate.
Dare I say more? Protect me, if you will,
Make me forget my grievance and be still,
And if I'm dear yet to your heart and eyes,
Go, win this duel in which I am the prize.
Farewell; I blush at having spoken so.

DON RODRIGUE

(*Alone.*)

Now I've the strength to conquer any foe:
Come, Moors, Castilians, Navarrese, each strain
Of fighting men that has been bred in Spain;
Be joined into an army now, and try
To overcome one man inspired as I;
Yes, try in vain to make my sweet hopes fail;
For all your thousands, you shall not prevail.

[*Le Cid*]

Scene Two

The Infanta

THE INFANTA

Shall I pay heed, still, to the voice of pride,
 Which views my passion with disdain?
Or shall I let love's sweetness be my guide,
And overthrow that haughty tyrant's reign?
 Poor princess! How, between those twain
 Shall you be able to decide?
You are my peer, Rodrigue, through what you've done,
And yet, alas, you're not a prince's son.

Pitiless Fortune, need you separate
 My royal pride and my desire?
Must I be torn between my high estate
And him whose noble virtues I admire?
 How many sorrows, keen and dire,
 My sighing heart must now await,
While groping for what means it can discover
To quell my love, or else accept my lover!

Enough of this: my reason was misled,
 If it could scorn a man so fine.
Though it's to wed a king that I was bred,
I'd live in honor, Rodrigue, if you were mine.

You've conquered kings, and that's a sign
    That soon a crown will grace your head;
And that great title, Cid, which now you gain
Points to the kingdom where you are to reign.

He's worthy of me, and yet that cannot be.
    Alas, I gave him to Chimène.
Her father's death caused no such enmity
As could prevent their joining hands again.
    I cannot hope to profit, then,
    By his crime, or my agony,
Since Fate, to punish me, has chosen to show
How love can last, even twixt foe and foe.

[*Le Cid*]

Scene Three

The Infanta, Léonor

THE INFANTA

What is it, Léonor?

LÉONOR

I'm glad, madame,
That once again your spirits can be calm.

THE INFANTA

How should that be, when I am racked with woe?

LÉONOR

Love lives on hope, and dies when hope must go.
Rodrigue cannot now fuel your desires,
For through this duel that Chimène requires
He'll either die or he shall wed Chimène.
Your hopes are dead; your mind's at peace again.

THE INFANTA

Ah, no; not yet!

LÉONOR

What hope, then, have you got?

Say rather, what resources have I not?
If under those alternatives he fights,
I know some schemes for putting things to rights.
Love, the sweet source of all my cruel pains,
Teaches a thousand tricks to lovers' brains.

LÉONOR

What can you do, though, if a father dead
Could not estrange two spirits all but wed?
Chimène has made it clear for all to see
That it's not hate that motivates her plea.
She's asked for combat, and was quick to take
Don Sanche's bid to battle for her sake,
Not waiting to enlist some other knight
Seasoned in warfare and renowned in fight.
As for Don Sanche, he could not please her more,
Since he has never drawn his sword before.
His youth and inexperience combined
Appeal to her, and give her peace of mind;
Thus she has staged, by choosing with such skill,
A duel that seems to override her will,
A combat that will seemingly appease
Her honor, and that Rodrigue will win with ease.

THE INFANTA

I know as much, and yet I must adore,
As rival to Chimène, this conqueror.
Sad lover that I am, what shall I do?

LÉONOR

Remember who it was that fathered you.
You love a subject! God means you for a king.

[*Le Cid*]

I've changed the object of my coveting.
No more do I love Rodrigue, a simple knight.
Ah, no, he's altered in my amorous sight:
I love the brilliant strokes his sword has wielded,
I love the Cid, to whom two kings have yielded.
Yet I'll suppress my heart, not fearing blame
But lest I mar their love's delightful flame;
And even if he received the crown I crave
For him, I'd not take back what once I gave.
He'll surely win this duel; let us then
Bestow Rodrigue once more upon Chimène;
Come: you, who know my griefs as no one can,
Shall see me finish what I once began.

Scene Four

Chimène, Elvire

CHIMÈNE

How I am suffering! Pity me, Elvire.
I don't know what to hope. I'm full of fear.
Whatever I long for makes me cry alack.
Whatever I wish, I quickly take it back.
On my account, two men must fight a duel:
Whatever the outcome, I shall find it cruel.
Whatever happens, I foresee with dread
A father unavenged, or a lover dead.

ELVIRE

In any event, your trials will soon be done:
You'll have Rodrigue, or vengeance will be won.
Whatever Fate decides, you shall have gained
A husband, and your honor been sustained.

CHIMÈNE

What! Him I hate, or that more hateful other!
The killer of Rodrigue, or of my father!
In either case, I'd be the partner of
A man who'd spilled the blood of one I love.
At either thought my soul rebels, and I
Can't face this duel's end. I'd rather die.

[Le Cid]

Away then, Love and Vengeance! You exhaust
My spirit; I'll not have you at such cost.
And you, almighty Fate who torture me,
Pray end this fight without a victory;
Let neither man be beaten or prevail.

That would but give you further cause to wail.
This duel could mean for you a fresh ordeal
If, when it ended, you must still appeal
For justice, be consumed with anger still,
And hound your lover, seeking for the kill.
Far better that the laurels on his brow
Should triumph, and your pleas be silenced now;
That your sighs cease, as honor's law requires,
And the king bid you follow your desires.

CHIMÈNE

If he should win, must I capitulate?
My duty is too strong, my loss too great,
And it would take far more to silence me
Than laws of combat or the king's decree.
Rodrigue can best Don Sanche with ease, but then
He won't disarm the honor of Chimène;
Despite the promise that the king has made,
I'll call a thousand champions to my aid.

ELVIRE

Be careful lest the heavens make you pay
For this outrageous pride that you display.
Come! Shall you scorn an opportunity
To keep your honor and withdraw your plea?
What does this duty of yours intend to do?

[Act Five / Scene Four]   109

Can a lover's death restore a sire to you?
Is it not enough to bear one bitter blow?
Must you have loss on loss, and woe on woe?
Lord! Banish these fantastic notions, or
You won't deserve the man you're destined for,
And we'll see Heaven, properly irate,
Destroy Rodrigue and make Don Sanche your mate.

CHIMÈNE

Elvire, I've griefs enough to trouble me;
Don't double them by such an augury.
I wish that neither man would win the day;
If that can't be, it's for Rodrigue I pray:
Not that an anxious love inclines me so,
But if he lost, Don Sanche would win, you know,
And all my hope is based upon that fear.
But what do I see? All hope is lost, Elvire.

Scene Five

Don Sanche, Chimène, Elvire

DON SANCHE

Laying this sword before you, I've obeyed —

CHIMÈNE

Is Rodrigue's blood still wet upon its blade?
Villain, how dare you show your features here,
Now that you've murdered what I held most dear?
Speak out, my heart, you've nothing more to hide:
Speak freely, for my father's satisfied.
One blow has saved my honor, foundered me
In deepest woe, and set my passion free.

DON SANCHE

If you'll be calm, my lady . . .

CHIMÈNE

                  You dare say more,
Vile butcher of the hero I adore!
You won by trickery: a knight so brave
Would never have succumbed to such a knave.
Don't think you've served me; I've no debt to you.
You thought to avenge me, but 'twas I you slew.

DON SANCHE

Do listen to me, madam. I entreat—

CHIMÈNE

You'd have me hear you boast of his defeat,
And listen patiently while you dilate
Upon my crime, your courage, and his fate?

[*Le Cid*]

Scene Six:
The Royal Court

Chimène, Don Diègue, Don Fernand,
Don Sanche, Don Arias, Don Alonse, Elvire

CHIMÈNE

Sire, there's no need now to deny anew
What all my efforts could not hide from you:
I loved him, as you saw, but had to take
Revenge upon him for my father's sake.
Your Majesty, indeed, was witness of
The way my duty had eclipsed my love.
But now Rodrigue is dead, and I am left
His foe no longer, but a heart bereft.
I owed that vengeance to a father slain,
And to my love I owe these tears of pain.
Don Sanche has been my murderous champion,
And I'm the prize for what his arm has done!
Sire, if you can be moved to pity, pray
Revoke the harsh decree you spoke today;
I'll leave him, for this costly victory,
All that I own; but let him leave me free
To dwell within a convent, and to cry
For sire and lover there until I die.

DON DIÈGUE

Well, sire, she loves my son, and feels that now
It is a truth she freely can avow.

DON FERNAND

Chimène, be undeceived; Rodrigue's not dead.
Don Sanche was beaten; by him, you've been misled.

DON SANCHE

Sire, she mistook me, being overwrought:
I came to see her, once our duel was fought.
The noble knight by whom her heart is charmed
Had nobly spared me, once I was disarmed.
"I cannot spill your blood," he told me, "when
That blood was risked in service to Chimène.
But since my duty calls me to the king,
Go in my name and tell her everything,
And lay your sword as trophy at her feet."
Alas, that sword resulted in deceit:
She thought I had returned as victor, sire,
And showed her love by sudden rage and fire,
By such a storm of grief that not a word
Of what I meant to tell her could be heard.
Though I have lost at arms, I am content,
And though my passion's vain, I'll not lament,
But rather shall rejoice in a defeat
That makes way for a love so strong and sweet.

DON FERNAND

Daughter, don't blush for what is now made plain,
Nor seek to hide your feelings, which in vain
Your modesty still urges you to do.

[*Le Cid*]

Your duty's done; your honor's bright anew;
You have avenged your father, for whose sake
Rodrigue has had such mortal risks to take.
Heaven has saved him; let yourself have one
Blessing from Heaven, after all you've done,
And don't rebel, my dear, at my command
That you bestow, on him you love, your hand.

Scene Seven

The Infanta, Don Rodrigue, Chimène, Don Fernand,
Don Diègue, Don Arias, Don Alonse, Don Sanche, Léonor, Elvire

THE INFANTA

Chimène, your princess bids you to receive
This hero from my hands, and cease to grieve.

DON RODRIGUE

Forgive me, sire, if in your court I kneel
To show her the respect and love I feel.
I have not come to claim a prize, Chimène:
I'm here to offer you my head again.
Lady, I shall not cite in this my plea
The laws of combat or the king's decree.
If all I've done has not avenged your sire,
Tell me what satisfactions you require.
Must I confront a thousand rivals more,
Extend my fame to Earth's remotest shore,
Eclipse the fabled heroes of the past,
And with my sword make armies flee aghast?
If through such feats my crime can be forgot,
I'll undertake them and achieve the lot;
But if your fiery honor and your pride
Cannot without my death be satisfied,
Don't send against me any human foes:

[Le Cid]

Your hands must take my life, for only those
Could hope to vanquish the invincible
And turn this offered head into a skull.
Pray let my death suffice to punish me,
And do not ban me from your memory,
But keep me in your heart, and so requite
A vengeance that will keep your honor bright,
Saying of me at times, with some regret,
"Had he not loved me, he'd be living yet."

CHIMÈNE

Arise, Rodrigue. Sire, I cannot undo
The love I feel, and have confessed to you.
Rodrigue's high virtues I cannot gainsay,
And when a king commands, one should obey.
And yet, whatever you have once decreed,
Can you permit this marriage to proceed?
If I obey your orders, as I must,
Shall that compulsion seem entirely just?
If Rodrigue is now essential to the State,
Must I, for salary, become his mate,
And bear an endless guilt because the stains
Upon my hands are from my father's veins?

DON FERNAND

Often, what seemed at first to be a crime
Has come to be acceptable in time.
Rodrigue has won you; you are his, and though
Upon this day his valor made you so,
I would abuse your honor if I placed
Your hand in his with an unfeeling haste.
We shall defer the marriage. My words still stand,
And you shall wed, in time, by my command.

[Act Five / Scene Seven]   117

Take, if you wish, a year to dry your tears.
For you, Rodrigue, another battle nears.
Now that you've thrown the Moors' invasion back,
Foiling their plans and stemming their attack,
Carry the war to them, taking command
Of all my forces, and lay waste their land.
The name of Cid will set them quivering;
They've called you lord, they'll want you for their king.
But mid these deeds, remain her faithful lover;
Return, if may be, still more worthy of her,
After such splendid exploits that for pride
And honor's sake she'll gladly be your bride.

DON RODRIGUE

To win Chimène, to serve the State and you,
What labors are there that I could not do?
Though to be far from her will mean distress,
That I can hope will be my happiness.

DON FERNAND

Trust in your valor and my promise, then,
And since you're loved already by Chimène,
Hope that this scruple, to which we see her cling,
Will yield to time, to courage, and your king.

The LIAR

1643

Introduction

P IERRE CORNEILLE WROTE *The Liar* — a free adaptation of a Spanish play by Alarcón — during the winter of 1643–44, and it was then performed at Paris's Théâtre du Marais, with the famous comedian Jodelet in the role of Cliton. It was a hit, and we are told that Parisian ladies, charmed by Dorante's imagined banquet-on-the-water in Act One, clamored for real entertainments based upon "la fête du *Menteur*." The verve and inventiveness of the play have continued to delight audiences ever since.

It is a dishonorable thing to tell a lie, and the point is vigorously made by Dorante's friend Alcippe, who lays it down that "Deceit was never taught in valor's school," as well as by Géronte, Dorante's father, in his furious reproaches of Act Five. Corneille himself said that Dorante's fictions "are certainly not good from a moral point of view." And it is not only for mendacity that Dorante might be faulted; one cannot admire, for instance, his callow disrespect for a patient and loving father. Nevertheless the audience of this play, or its reader, does not anticipate some sort of punishment or bitter come-uppance for the hero. *The Liar* is not experienced as a moral fable; it is animated by something else.

In the very first speech of the play, Dorante declares that he has "doffed the Robe and donned the Sword," and asks his valet, Cliton, whether his appearance as a dashing cavalier is convincing. Cliton reassures him, and goes on to describe Paris as a city in which each newcomer is free to invent himself—a city, as Géronte later says, in which "metamorphoses are everywhere." From the beginning, *The Liar* projects, not only in Dorante but in its whole atmosphere and action, a baroque sense of the world's duplicity, a dazzling texture of appearance and reality. One finds this theme in Alcippe's blind mistakenness and Cliton's repeated deception; in Clarice's speech (Act Two, Scene Two) about the difficulty of divining a suitor's true nature; in Clarice's twilight impersonation of Lucrèce, in which Lucrèce abets her; in the calculating demureness of Sabine; in Géronte's urgent belief in the fictitious Orphise and Armédon. Of being and seeming, truth and falsehood, there is no end in this play. By Act Three, the texture of true-and-false has grown so dense that Clarice can say of Dorante that "He makes a fib sound honest and naive, / So that one's almost tempted to believe." Later in the same act, that ambiguity is inverted: Dorante is distressed that his "honest passion" has not been believed, and cries, "I told the truth." To which Cliton replies, "Yes, but a liar said it, / And coming from your lips it lost all credit."

However wrong it is to speak falsely, critics have pointed out that Dorante's lies are not base or mean; most of them are intended, as Isabelle says, to show the liar as "Not what he is, but what he'd like to be"— a famous soldier, a gallant and generous ladies' man, a speaker of ten languages, and so on. Dorante's invention of a forced marriage to "Orphise" is mitigated, so Corneille said, by the fact that his motive is love. In any case, the fact is that we listen to Dorante's fibs and fantasies with shock but also with pleasure, enjoying his quickness of mind and inventive amplitude, and hearing in his bold speeches something not wholly unlike the heroic vaunts of Corneille's tragic heroes.

In another baroque comedy of Corneille's, *L'Illusion comique* (1637), there is a boastful soldier named Matamore whose conversation consists entirely of whopping lies regarding his prowess and his conquests. Matamore is delightful, yet since no one in the play ever believes him, he has little impact on the plot. The lies of Dorante, however, do have consequences, and they, together with his confusion between Lucrèce and Clarice, initiate a comedy of intrigue that builds to a crisis of bewilderment in Act Five, Scene Six. The next and final scene settles everything in a blithe, conventional, and slightly bittersweet manner, marrying everyone off in spite of doubts and reservations.

In proportion to his presence on stage, we do not understand a great deal about Dorante; Clarice and Lucrèce are not analyzed in depth; Géronte is to some extent a stock figure; it may be that Cliton — cynical, witty, worldly-wise, and annoyed at being taken in — is the most fully developed character in *The Liar*. Yet one can easily understand the younger Molière's reported admiration for the play, and one can see how it may have pointed the way to those great comedies of character in which Molière studies the impact of a quirky central figure on those around him. Certainly the fifth act of Molière's *Don Juan*, in which Don Luis berates his degenerate son, is much indebted to Géronte's upbraidings of Dorante.

But *The Liar* is in itself a marvel, and need not be enhanced by claims for its influence. I hope that my translation has done it justice, and I thank my wife for patiently reading it as it came.

R. W.
Cummington, 2007

The LIAR

1643

Cast of Characters

GÉRONTE, father of Dorante

DORANTE, Géronte's son

ALCIPPE, friend of Dorante, suitor of Clarice

PHILISTE, friend of Alcippe and Dorante

CLARICE, a young woman courted by Alcippe

LUCRÈCE, a young woman, friend of Clarice

ISABELLE, Clarice's maid

SABINE, Lucrèce's maid

CLITON, Dorante's valet

LYCAS, Alcippe's valet

THE SCENE

Paris

The names of the characters should be pronounced
in a more-or-less French manner, as follows:

DORANTE	do-RAHNT
ALCIPPE	ahl-SEEP
CLARICE	clah-REECE
LUCRÈCE	loo-CRESS
CLITON	clee-TAWN

ACT ONE

Scene One

Dorante, Cliton

DORANTE

At last I've doffed the Robe and donned the Sword;
This is the life that I've been yearning toward;
Father has let me follow my desire,
And so I've thrown my law books on the fire.
But since we're in the Tuileries today,
Where style and gallantry are on display,
Do I appear a gay young blade to you,
Or does the grubby scholar still show through?
One doesn't learn from any legal book
What one must do to have a dashing look.
I fear I may not—

CLITON

        Ah, sir, have no fear:
You'll soon have many jealous rivals here.

Your looks do not suggest a law school drudge,
Or Bartolus, that venerable judge.
I sense that many a husband will dislike you.
But tell me now, sir: how does Paris strike you?

DORANTE

The air is sweeter here, and that I've spent
Dull months on law I bitterly lament.
But you who've lived here always — have you not? —
Know where the city's pleasures may be got:
What does one do for ladies' company?

CLITON

Ah, that's the sweetest pleasure that can be:
So say the poets. Not to be impolite,
You have, sir, a most eager appetite.
Only last night you came to town, and yet
An idle morning makes you chafe and fret!
You're on the move already, and you aim
To try your hand at love's delightful game!
Well, as it happens, I am qualified
In that regard to be your coach and guide.
I'm master of that trade, with high renown
As chief arranger in this part of town.

DORANTE

Don't take offense, now. All I want, you see,
Is a lady friend who'll laugh a bit with me,
In whose sweet company I can be gay
And let a charming hour slip away.
Not knowing me, you made a slight mistake.

CLITON

I understand you, sir. You're not a rake,
And you'd despise the sort of woman who
Yields all her favors for a coin or two.
No more would you desire those cold coquettes
From whom flirtatious looks are all one gets,
And who make love by naughty word and wink;
A man like you wants something more, I think.
Time is not spent but lost with such as they;
The game's not worth the candle, as they say.
No, where you'll find the happiness you crave
Is with good wives who sometimes misbehave,
Women whose virtue's not so strict and nice
As to deny itself a little vice.
We have them here in all varieties,
But do not ask me how to meet them, please;
Unless, sir, I have read your face amiss,
You're not a novice in affairs like this;
I'm sure the study of law did not demand
That you always keep a briefcase in your hand.

DORANTE

Frankly, Cliton, I must confess to you
That in Poitiers I lived as young men do:
There was no role or game I didn't play.
But Paris is a long way from Poitiers.
The difference in styles is very great.
What there is modish, here is out of date.
Trying to act and speak like a Parisian,
A stranger is an object of derision.
Out in the provinces, we're laissez-faire,

[Act One / Scene One]   131

And any sort of fool's accepted there,
But Paris asks for finer qualities,
And flashy ostentation fails to please;
To be received here, one must take one's cue
From the gentry who are everywhere on view.

CLITON

Paris is not so simple, you will find.
It's a big place full of folk of every kind.
Not everything you see can be believed,
And, just as elsewhere, one can be deceived.
Mixed in with fine and decent folk are louts
And rogues aplenty, thieves and layabouts.
To the great whirlpool of this city come
From every town its worthies and its scum,
And all of France — from north, east, south, and west —
Sends to this capital its worst and best.
Each new, unknown arrival can elect
The style of life that suits his self-respect,
And worse than you have proven sterling men.
But now, to address your question once again:
Are you the generous kind?

DORANTE

I'm not a miser.

CLITON

That attitude, in love, could not be wiser.
But, sir, we must be artful when we spend.
If not, we just lose money in the end.
Some get no thanks, though spending great amounts;
It's how you give, not what you give, that counts.
Some slyly lose at cards; some leave behind

Chez elle a brooch that would have been declined;
A lumpish lover fills his mistress' palms
With costly things that seem not gifts but alms,
And that munificence, however tender,
By its excess does nothing but offend her.

DORANTE

Forget those lumpish lovers now, and say
That you know the two young ladies bound this way.

CLITON

No, no, they're goods of choicest quality;
They're game reserved for others, not for me.
But I can check upon them, as it were:
Their coachman will be glad to brief me, sir.

DORANTE

He will?

CLITON

Of course; he'll brief me till I drop.
Coachmen are folk who talk and never stop.

Scene Two

Clarice, Dorante, Lucrèce, Isabelle

CLARICE

(*Stumbling and almost falling.*)

Oh!

DORANTE

(*Giving her his hand.*)
Madam, I bless the mishap that has made
It possible for me to lend you aid.
It's a happy chance that gives me an excuse
To offer you my hand, and be of use.

CLARICE

It's a very little mishap that you bless,
And a slight cause indeed for happiness.

DORANTE

It's true, I owe it all to accident,
Rather than your desire or my intent,
Which makes me sadly see that Fate did not
Intend this happiness to be my lot.

[*The Liar*]

No, my unworthy self could never be
Accorded such a great felicity.

If joy so quickly has forsaken you,
Allow me to express a different view.
No happiness is sweeter, I submit,
Than to be glad without deserving it.
I better like a gift than a reward,
For gifts give more than justice can afford,
And the greatest joy that worthiness can get
Is no more than the payment of a debt.
The favor we deserve is always bought;
Felicity is greater when unsought,
And that delight we effortlessly gain
Merit must struggle for and not obtain.

DORANTE

Don't think that I expect to know the bliss
Of meriting so great a joy as this;
My fond heart knows its rarity, and the less
My merit is, the more my happiness.
Your favor was denied me in the past,
And if my heart, receiving it at last,
Complains, it is of one thing lacking still—
That chance bestows it, rather than your will.
A lover can't be perfectly content
When favors that are shown him are not meant,
Because intention is the germ and key
Without which actions are but mockery.
Judge then if my love's flame is satisfied

When a hand is given, but a heart denied.
I hold this hand, I touch it, but in vain:
I cannot touch your heart in its disdain.

CLARICE

This flame of yours, sir, takes me by surprise,
Kindling so suddenly before my eyes.
If your heart feels combustion at first sight,
My own, I fear, is slower to ignite.
But now that you've informed me, it may be
That time will bring a greater sympathy.
Meanwhile, admit that you were wrong to scold me
For scorning love of which you hadn't told me.

Scene Three

Dorante, Clarice, Cliton, Lucrèce, Isabelle

DORANTE

Yes, that's the bad luck that's been hounding me
Since I returned from war in Germany;
That is to say, I've spent at least a year
Haunting, both day and night, your quarter here,
Looking for you at balls or promenades,
Devoting to you many serenades,
Yet never had a chance till now to say
The heartfelt words that I have said today.

CLARICE

You've been at war in Germany? Is that so?

DORANTE

For four long years I terrified the foe.

CLITON

What is he saying?

DORANTE

                          And during those four years
There was no siege, no charge of cavaliers,

No clash from which our arms emerged victorious,
In which the part I played was less than glorious.
In the *Gazette*, my prowess was enshrined . . .

Are you aware, sir, that you've lost your mind?

DORANTE

Be still.

CLITON

You're dreaming, or —

DORANTE

              Be still, I said.

CLITON

You came from Poitiers, or God strike me dead.
You got here yesterday.

DORANTE

              Be still, you beast.
        (*To Clarice.*)
My role in all our victories increased
Until, it's fair to say, I had some fame,
And I would still be in that manly game
Had I not come to court last winter, where
I saw you, and was conquered then and there.
Your eyes unmanned me; I laid down my arms;
I was a prisoner of your many charms;
My soul surrendered, and this noble heart
Forgot all other wishes from the start.
To win great battles, gallantly to lead,

To swell my fame by many a famous deed,
All those desires I'd harbored thitherto
Gave way now to my joy in serving you.

ISABELLE

(*To Clarice, sotto voce.*)
Madame, Alcippe is coming; he'll be vexed.

CLARICE

We'll hear some more, sir, when we see you next.
Farewell.

DORANTE

You'll go, and leave me joyless here?

CLARICE

We have no time for further talk, I fear.
Delightful as your flatteries are, please pardon
Our leaving now to stroll about the garden.

DORANTE

Then, till we meet again, I beg you to
Permit my smitten heart to worship you.

CLARICE

If a heart would love, and knows how that is done,
It need not ask for leave from anyone.

Scene Four

Dorante, Cliton

DORANTE

Follow those two.

CLITON

        I've found out where they live.
The coachman was, as usual, talkative.
His mistress is the prettier of the pair.
Her name's Lucrèce; she lives here on the square.

DORANTE

What square?

CLITON

        The Place Royale, sir, and the same
Goes for the other. He didn't know her name.

DORANTE

You needn't bother, Cliton, to find it out.
The one I talked with and am mad about
Is named Lucrèce; yes, that's her name, I know.
Her beauty and my heart both tell me so.

        [*The Liar*]

CLITON

I think, with all due deference to you,
That the other one's the prettier of the two.

DORANTE

You mean that witless one who didn't add
One word to the discussion that we had?

CLITON

When a woman has the gift of silence, sir,
No other of her sex can equal her.
It is a boon from Heaven, which without
A miracle could not be brought about:
When Heaven moves a woman to be quiet,
The laws of Nature are suspended by it.
Love's not a thing for which I sigh and bleed;
I go and get some when I feel the need;
But when a woman knows how to be still
I feel for her such passionate goodwill
That even if she's plain and poorly dressed
She has my vote for loveliest and best.
I know which one's Lucrèce. Keep asking, sir,
And we'll learn the name of her whom you prefer.
It's Lucrèce who didn't speak. And strike me dead
If she's not the prettier, as the coachman said.

DORANTE

No need for oaths; it may be as you say.
But look, two dear old friends are bound this way.
Something's excited them, to say the least.

Scene Five

Philiste, Alcippe, Cliton, Dorante

PHILISTE

(*To Alcippe.*)

What! Music on the waters, and then a feast?

ALCIPPE

(*To Philiste.*)

A feast, with music playing all the time.

PHILISTE

(*To Alcippe.*)

Last night?

ALCIPPE

(*To Philiste.*)

Last night.

PHILISTE

(*To Alcippe.*)

What was it like?

ALCIPPE

(*To Philiste.*)

Sublime.

[*The Liar*]

PHILISTE

(*To Alcippe.*)
Who gave this fête?

ALCIPPE

(*To Philiste.*)
Well, that's what isn't clear.

DORANTE

(*Greeting them.*)
Friends, what a joy it is to see you here!

ALCIPPE

Old friend, I feel a similar delight.

DORANTE

I interrupted you. 'Twas impolite.
But when I saw you I was rapturous.

PHILISTE

Nothing you do could give offense to us.

DORANTE

What were you speaking of?

ALCIPPE

A gallant deed.

DORANTE

A deed of love?

ALCIPPE

Presumably.

[*Act One / Scene Five*]   143

DORANTE

Please proceed,
And since I'm curious, please let me share
In your description of this fine affair.

ALCIPPE

A lady was given a concert, so they claim.

DORANTE

On the water?

ALCIPPE

Yes.

DORANTE

The waves can fan love's flame.

ALCIPPE

No doubt.

DORANTE

And this took place last night?

ALCIPPE

Last night.

DORANTE

Darkness can make the flame of love burn bright.
Well timed. Is the lady beautiful, or no?

ALCIPPE

Most people, I believe, would think her so.

[*The Liar*]

DORANTE

And the music?

ALCIPPE

Decent; not to be derided.

DORANTE

And was some sort of splendid meal provided?

ALCIPPE

They say so.

DORANTE

Lavish?

ALCIPPE

And wondrous good to eat.

DORANTE

And you don't know who gave this princely treat?

ALCIPPE

You're laughing. Why?

DORANTE

I laugh to hear you rave
About a little banquet that I gave.

ALCIPPE

You?

DORANTE

I.

You've already found someone to court?

DORANTE

If not, my efforts would have fallen short.
I've been in town now for a month-long stay.
It's true, I seldom venture out by day;
At night, I go about incògnito.
That's why —

CLITON

(*To Dorante, in a whisper.*)
Oh, sir! That's just not true, you know.

DORANTE

Be still! If once again you dare deny . . .

CLITON

I hate to hold my tongue and hear him lie.

PHILISTE

(*To Alcippe, sotto voce.*)
What luck to meet your rival, and to hear
Him give away his game in terms so clear.

DORANTE

(*Turning back to them.*)
Dear friends, I'll tell you everything I can.
I hired five boats to implement my plan.
The first four held musicians who could play
So sweetly as to drive all gloom away.
In the first were violins; voices and lutes
Came next; then oboes; in the fourth were flutes,

And all these in their turn contrived to please
The ravished ear with airy harmonies.
The fifth boat was quite large; I had it decked
With interwoven boughs to good effect,
And at the bow and stern were massed bouquets
Of orange, jasmine, and pomegranate sprays.
I made that boat into our banquet hall,
And led aboard the one who is my all;
Four other beauties were her maiden chorus,
And soon a choice repast was set before us.
I shall not tell you everything we ate —
What sauce was served, the name of every plate;
I'll tell you only this, that twelve delicious
Courses were eaten, each with six fine dishes.
Meanwhile the air re-echoed with the notes
Of water music from the first four boats.
Thousands of rockets, when our meal was through,
Rose in the sky, straight upward or askew,
And turned the night to day, and crumbled so
Their flames upon the water's face below,
It seemed that all the fires of Heaven bore
Down on the Earth in elemental war.
That pastime over, we danced until the dawn,
Which the Sun, that jealous god, brought swiftly on;
Had he been tractable and opportune,
He'd not have shown his face so very soon;
But, having more than our desires in sight,
He rose, and put an end to our delight.

ALCIPPE

You tell these wonders with a charming air.
Paris is large, but such events are rare.

[Act One / Scene Five]   147

DORANTE

'Twas planned in haste. The one whom I adore
Gave me two hours' warning, and no more.

PHILISTE

Still, it was lavish, and superbly planned.

DORANTE

One had to settle for what came to hand.
When time is short, one cannot pick and choose.

ALCIPPE

We'll meet again, old friend, and share our news.

DORANTE

Agreed, old friend.

ALCIPPE

(*To Philiste, as they leave.*)
I'm sick with jealousy.

PHILISTE

Jealous? I think you have no cause to be,
For his account and yours don't seem to fit.

ALCIPPE

The place and time do, and that settles it.

Scene Six

Cliton, Dorante

CLITON

Sir, may I speak now without vexing you?

DORANTE

Speak or be still; I don't care which you do.
But further insolence is not allowed.

CLITON

Is it your habit, sir, to dream out loud?

DORANTE

What do you mean by "dream"?

CLITON

By a dream, sir, I
Mean what, in someone else, would be a lie.

DORANTE

Hush, muddle-head.

CLITON

It muddles me the more
To hear you speak of concerts and of war.

[Act One / Scene Six]   149

You fight our battles at no risk to you,
And give great banquets that don't cost a sou.
Why claim, sir, that you've been in town a year?

DORANTE

To show my love as lasting and sincere.

CLITON

How does this war talk help to prove your love?

DORANTE

Think how a lady'd be enamoured of
A suitor who declared, "I bring to thee
A heart fresh from the University!
If thou hast need of rubrics and of laws,
I know Justinian's codex, clause by clause,
And Baldus, and Accursius' glosses too,
And the latest issue of the *Law Review*."
Yes, *there's* the sort of speech that can impart
Style to a man, and melt the coldest heart!
Law student is indeed a brave profession!
But a soldier makes a better first impression.
All that's required is just a bit of sham—
To lie unblinkingly, to say goddamn,
To use words unfamiliar to the fair,
To talk of generals like Jean de Vert
And German castles, each of which can claim
A barbarous, unutterable name,
To speak of sectors, counterscarps, front lines,
Detachments, ditches, bastions, flanks, and mines.
No need to make a particle of sense;
The ladies will be stunned by your pretense,

And you will manage through your little lies
To be a striking figure in their eyes.

CLITON

A lady might well hear you and not doubt you,
But she might very soon find out about you.

DORANTE

By then I should have known her for a time,
And she'd not see my fictions as a crime:
Indeed, if we were cornered by a bore,
We'd make our secret code from terms of war.
That, Cliton, is my amorous strategy.

CLITON

To tell the truth, sir, you're too much for me.
But let's discuss that feast. The Fairy Queen
Never so quickly made such fine cuisine.
You've outdone all her spells and sorceries.
You could write novels with enchanting ease.
Your heroes, since your fancy is so fecund,
Could gallop round the earth in half a second,
And you could readily provide a page
Of thrills or luxury at every stage.
You have a gift for stunning fabrications.

DORANTE

That's how I deal with bores who hawk sensations.
When I perceive that someone means to tell me
A piece of news he thinks will overwhelm me,
I tell him an outrageous tale so choice
That sheer amazement robs him of his voice.

[*Act One / Scene Six*]   151

It's a great pleasure, through that little ruse,
To see a prattler swallowing his news.

CLITON

No doubt it is, although behaving so
Can get you into bitter scrapes, you know.

DORANTE

Well, I'll get out of them. But why postpone
My quest for her I hope to call my own?
Let's try to find her. Come, and let me give
You further lessons, now, in how to live.

ACT TWO

Scene One

Clarice, Géronte, Isabelle

CLARICE

That he's a son of yours, sir, is no mean
Attraction, yet to wed him sight unseen,
Though you assure me he's extraordinary,
Would show a strange anxiety to marry.
What's more, were he to call upon me, and
Be welcomed as a suitor for my hand,
Before your plan gave signs of working out,
'Twould give the world too much to talk about.
Pray find some way for me to see your son
In which no risk of scandal will be run.

GÉRONTE

Clarice, you are both beautiful and wise,
And I shall gladly do as you advise.
Bowing in this to your authority,
I'll soon return, and bring Dorante with me.

Beneath your window I'll detain him, so
That you can look him over, high and low.
Study his form, his face, his bearing too,
And judge what kind of spouse I offer you.
He's fresh from Poitiers, but I think that you'll
Agree that he's not redolent of school.
Young scholar though he is, he likes to sport
Clothes as well cut as anyone's at court.
But judge him, too, by the decent life he's led.
He's my only son; I long to see him wed,
And dearly hope that you will be his bride.

CLARICE

By that sweet wish I'm deeply gratified.
I'm eager for a better knowledge òf him,
And even now your words have made me love him.

[The Liar]

Scene Two

Isabelle, Clarice

ISABELLE
So, uncommitted, you'll look this fellow over.

CLARICE
But, from a window, what can I discover?
I'll see his mien, his looks, his outward show,
But, Isabelle, of the rest what can I know?
Faces are flattering mirrors that provide
Untrue reflections of the man inside;
How many flaws can lurk behind a smile!
And handsomeness can hide a soul that's vile.
Choosing a husband, we must use our eyes,
Yet trusting them alone is most unwise.
If we're to be happy, what they see must please them;
Though not obeying, we must yet appease them;
We must accept their *no* but not their *yes*,
And build on firmer ground our happiness.
This marriage bond, which lasts our life entire,
And which should cause more terror than desire,
Unless one's careful, often seems to wed
Like to unlike, the living to the dead.
Since marriage means to have a master, I

Must know the man I'm to be mastered by,
Ere I accept him.

ISABELLE

Then he must talk with you.

CLARICE

Alcippe would be most jealous if he knew.

ISABELLE

What do you care? Dorante's the better bet.

CLARICE

I'm not prepared to lose Alcippe as yet.
We pledged to marry, and if affairs permit
His sire to come here, I'll go through with it.
For two years now his father has delayed;
Sometimes it's business, sometimes he's afraid
Of stormy weather, or the roads are poor.
The dear man clearly wants to stay in Tours.
In these delays I read mistrust of me,
And I don't aim to die of constancy.
Each minute that we wait brings down our price;
Young virgins can grow older in a trice;
Theirs is a title that, if kept, brings shame;
The timely loss of it must be their aim.
They cannot fence with Time, which is too strong;
Their honor's lost if it's preserved too long.

ISABELLE

So, you might leave Alcippe, if you could find
Another who could please your heart and mind?

CLARICE

Yes, I might leave him, but do understand
That I'd have to have that other well in hand,
And think him right for me, and that the day
He married me could not be far away.
Without these things, my interest would be small.
Alcippe is better than nothing, after all;
His father, after all, may come to town.

ISABELLE

There's a safe way to nail this matter down.
Your friend Lucrèce is generous and zealous;
She has no suitors now who might be jealous;
Let her send Dorante a message to be right
Beneath her window on this very night.
Because he's young he'll take the dare, and you
And he may have a darkling interview;
And while Alcippe will never know the joke,
Dorante will think 'twas with Lucrèce he spoke.

CLARICE

A fine idea. Lucrèce will without question
Send him a sweet note, following your suggestion.
I much admire you for this cunning plan.

ISABELLE

Once more, I wonder if that unknown man
You met today has waked in you some feeling.

CLARICE

Oh, heavens! If Dorante proved so appealing,
Alcippe would not be needed any more.

ISABELLE

Don't speak of him; he's coming.

CLARICE

What a bore!
Go, please, and tell Lucrèce of our design,
And ask her help in these affairs of mine.

Scene Three

Alcippe, Clarice

ALCIPPE

Clarice! Clarice! Oh, false, inconstant one!

CLARICE

(*Initially aside.*)
Can he have guessed what I just now have done?
Alcippe, what is it that's upset you so?

ALCIPPE

What is it, traitress? As if you didn't know!
Your conscience knows what heavy guilt it bears.

CLARICE

Do speak more softly. Father will come downstairs.

ALCIPPE

"Father will come downstairs." That's but a myth.
You have a father just to hush me with.
At night, on the river . . .

CLARICE

The river? Yes, go on.
What are you trying to say?

ALCIPPE

All night, till dawn.

CLARICE

Well?

ALCIPPE

You should blush!

CLARICE

Blush? Why, in Heaven's name?

ALCIPPE

Hearing those few words, you should die of shame!

CLARICE

Why should they make me die, as you suggest?

ALCIPPE

So! Hearing them, you dare to hear the rest?
Will you not blush, if I describe it all?

CLARICE

All what?

ALCIPPE

The whole appalling carnival.

CLARICE

I've no idea of what you mean, I swear.

[*The Liar*]

ALCIPPE

When I speak to you, your father's on the stair.
It's a clever trick, for which you have a talent.
But as for spending all night with your gallant . . .

CLARICE

Alcippe, are you crazy?

ALCIPPE

                    Not with love for you,
Now that I know the sort of thing you do.
Yes, when you feast and dance the night away
With a gallant lover till the break of day
(As just occurred) does your father know you're out?

CLARICE

What's this mysterious feast you rave about?

ALCIPPE

It's a recent mystery that's been solved, my sweet.
Next time, best choose a lover more discreet.
He's told me everything.

CLARICE

                    Who?

ALCIPPE

                    Dorante. My friend.

CLARICE

Dorante!

ALCIPPE

Go on; claim not to comprehend.

CLARICE

I've never met the man; it isn't true.

ALCIPPE

Didn't I see his father visiting you?
Ah, fickle creature! You spend, unfaithful one,
Days with the father, nighttimes with the son!

CLARICE

His father and mine were bosom friends of yore.

ALCIPPE

And is that what he came to see you for?
You know you're guilty, but you still talk back!
How can I make your obstinacy crack?

CLARICE

Alcippe, I wouldn't know the son by sight.

ALCIPPE

When last you saw him, it was darkest night.
Did he not hire for you four bands at least,
And in your honor give a wondrous feast —
Six courses of twelve dishes each, and more?
Did you then find his company a bore?
And when his fireworks lighted up all space,
Did you not have a chance to see his face;
And going home by dawnlight, when your dance

Was over, did you give his face a glance?
Have I said enough? Now show some shame, and blush.

CLARICE

All I can say to that is pish and tush.

ALCIPPE

What am I, then? A liar? Jealous? Mad?

CLARICE

Someone, I fear, has hoaxed you. You've been had.
Trust me, Alcippe.

ALCIPPE

No, spare me your evasions;
I know your dodges and your sly persuasions.
Farewell. Go, follow your Dorante, and love him.
Forsake Alcippe, and think no longer òf him.

CLARICE

Please listen to me.

ALCIPPE

Your father's on the stair.

CLARICE

No, he can't hear us, and he isn't there;
Listen, and I'll disprove this calumny.

ALCIPPE

No, I won't listen, unless you marry me —
Unless, while we await our marriage, you
Give me your promise and two kisses, too.

[Act Two / Scene Three]   163

CLARICE

To clear my honor, what is it you demand,
Alcippe?

ALCIPPE

Your pledge, two kisses, and your hand.

CLARICE

No more?

ALCIPPE

Make up your mind; don't make me wait.

CLARICE

Father is coming down now; it's too late.

Scene Four

Alcippe

ALCIPPE

Now that you're lost to me, come mock my pain,
And free me from my bonds by your disdain;
Help my rejected passion to congeal
Till a just wrath is all that I can feel.
I thirst for vengeance, and shall take your lover
A cold and vengeful heart, as he'll discover.
If he's a man of honor, you'll receive
This very day some cause to laugh or grieve;
Yes, ere my treasure's taken by my foe
May all his blood, and mine, be made to flow!
Here comes my rival, and his father too.
Old friendship yields now to a hate that's new.
At sight of him, that hatred grows more grim,
But here is not the place to challenge him.

Scene Five

Géronte, Dorante, Cliton

GÉRONTE

Let's pause a while, Dorante. We've rushed about
Till I am short of breath and quite worn out.
How great this city is, how nobly planned!

DORANTE

All Paris seems to me a fairyland.
I saw this morning an enchanted isle
Which was unpeopled then, yet in a while
Some new Amphìon, so it seemed, had made
Great buildings rise there, with no builder's aid.

GÉRONTE

Such metamorphoses are everywhere.
You see the same thing in the Pré-aux-Clercs,
And nothing in the world is oh'd and ah'd
More than the Palais Cardinal's façade.
It is as if a whole great town should float
Skyward by magic out of an ancient moat,
And by its cloud-high parapets implied
That gods, or kings at least, must dwell inside.
But now to business. You know you have my love?

[*The Liar*]

DORANTE

It is the thing, sir, that I'm proudest of.

GÉRONTE

Since you're my only child, and since, I fear,
You've entered on a perilous career,
In which the quest for martial glory drives
Young soldiers every day to risk their lives,
Before some mishap comes to you, and makes
You slow down somewhat, and apply the brakes,
I want you married.

DORANTE

(*Aside.*)
Lucrèce, how I adore you!

GÉRONTE

I have picked out a proper partner fòr you —
Fair, virtuous, and rich.

DORANTE

Oh, Father, take
A bit more time to choose, for mercy's sake.

GÉRONTE

I know her well. Clarice is good and sweet
As any girl her age you're like to meet.
Her father's been my closest friend forever.
The matter's settled.

DORANTE

Oh, sir, it makes me shiver
To think of burdening my young years thus!

GÉRONTE

You'll do as I say.

DORANTE

(*Initially aside.*)
I must be devious.
Sir, I have yet to prove myself, and wield
My sword arm with distinction in the field—

GÉRONTE

Before some other sword arm takes your life,
I want you, for my sake, to take a wife;
I want a grandson who will fill your place,
And prop my old age, and preserve our race.
In short, I wish it.

DORANTE

Alas, you're adamant.

GÉRONTE

You'll do as I command.

DORANTE

But, sir, I can't.

GÉRONTE

You can't, you say! How so?

DORANTE

Permit me, please,
To ask your pardon while I clasp your knees.
I'm—

GÉRONTE

What?

DORANTE

In Poitiers —

GÉRONTE

Stand up, now. Explain.

DORANTE

I'm married, sir. To hide the truth is vain.

GÉRONTE

Without my blessing!

DORANTE

It was done by force,
Which you've the power to annul, of course.
We were compelled to wed in consequence
Of a series of outrageous accidents —
If you only knew.

GÉRONTE

Come, tell me everything.

DORANTE

She's of good family, though she doesn't bring
As rich a dowry as you might prefer.

GÉRONTE

What's done is done. Well, tell me more of her.
Her name?

Orphise. And Armédon's her father.

GÉRONTE

One name's as unfamiliar as the other.
Go on.

DORANTE

    Soon after I arrived, I saw
A girl for whom the coldest heart would thaw.
Such were her charms, so brilliant was her gaze,
That she enslaved me by her gentle ways.
I sought therefore to meet her, and to please
By gifts and kindnesses and courtesies,
Till after six months' fervent courtship òf her
I was both her beloved and her lover.
She showed me secret favors — though nothing wrong —
And I so pressed my conquest that ere long
I'd tiptoe through her quarter, out of sight,
To chat with her for part of every night.
One night, when I'd just climbed into her chamber
(It was, I think, the second of September —
Yes, I was caught precisely on that date),
Her father had been dining out till late.
He comes home, knocks upon her door, and she
Grows pale, then finds a hiding place for me,
Opens the door, and with sly expertise
Enfolds the old man in a hug and squeeze,
So that he won't perceive her rumpled state.
He sits down; says it's time she had a mate,
And tells her of an offer he's received.
Needless to say, I'm anxious and aggrieved,
But she replies with great diplomacy,

        [*The Liar*]

Pleasing her father and yet soothing me.
Just when the old man says that it is time
To go, my pocket watch begins to chime!
He says to his daughter, who's at first struck dumb,
"Since when do you have a watch? From whom did it
    come?"
"Acaste, my cousin, sent it," she declares,
"Requesting me to take it for repairs.
There are no jewelers where he lives, you know.
It just chimed three half-hours in a row."
"Give it to me," he says, "I'll get it working."
She comes then to the alcove where I'm lurking,
I hand it to her, but to my despair
The watch chain tangles with the gun I wear,
And pulls the trigger, and a shot rings out.
You can imagine what that brings about.
Seemingly dead, she drops then to the floor;
Her father runs in terror to the door
And calls out "Help!" and "Murder!" in his dismay.
Two servants and his son soon block my way.
Enraged by my mischance, consumed with wrath,
Through those three men I start to hew a path,
When, in another one of fate's caprices,
The sword I'm wielding breaks into three pieces.
Disarmed thus, I retreat; Orphise, who's quite
Recovered now from her initial fright,
Yet has the energy that fears provide,
Slams shut the door, and locks us both inside.
Quickly, we heap up chests and chairs to make
A barricade for reinforcement's sake,
Thinking that such a rampart may delay
Their coming in, and somehow win the day.
But as we labor to avert our doom,

They break the wall down from a neighboring room,
And we are forced to parley and confer.
    (Here Clarice observes them from her window,
        while Lucrèce, with Isabelle beside her,
           does the same from hers.)

GÉRONTE

So, in plain French, you had to marry her.

DORANTE

I had been found alone with her, at night;
Her kin outnumbered me; she charmed me quite;
The scandal might be great, her honor lost;
If I refused, my head would be the cost.
The way in which she bravely took my part
Had added to the fervor of my heart.
Therefore, to save my life and her repute,
And render our contentment absolute,
I said what calmed the storm, as anyone
In my position surely would have done.
Say now if you'd prefer to see me perish
Or dwell in happiness with one I cherish.

GÉRONTE

No, no, I'm not so harsh as you suppose.
I well can understand the course you chose.
My love excuses you; your only wrong
Was to have kept it secret for so long.

DORANTE

Her want of money made me wed by stealth.

GÉRONTE

A father should not make too much of wealth.
She's well born, fair, and good, and as you tell,
You love each other; that's enough. Farewell.
I'll tell Clarice's father that we withdraw.

Scene Six

Dorante, Cliton

DORANTE

Well, how did you like it? Are you full of awe?
Didn't I dupe him? Wasn't my story apt?
In my place, some poor fool would have been trapped.
He would have started in to moan and whine
And then, with a broken heart, have toed the line.
Yes, lying is a useful form of wit.

CLITON

What? It wasn't true, sir?

DORANTE

               Not a word of it.
What you just heard was a bit of cleverness
Which saved my heart and soul for fair Lucrèce.

CLITON

And the watch, the sword, the pistol, what were they?

DORANTE

Inventions.

CLITON

Sir, oblige your poor valet.
When you're about to pull some masterstroke,
I wish you'd make me privy to the joke:
Though you'd forewarned me, I was taken in.

DORANTE

Henceforth, you'll share in all the lies I spin.
You'll be the secretary of my spirit,
And if I have a secret, you shall hear it.

CLITON

Since I'm to be so privileged, I'll hope
In serving you, to understand and cope.
What are your plans for amorous success?

Scene Seven

Sabine, Dorante, Cliton

SABINE
(*Handing Dorante a letter.*)
Read this, sir.

DORANTE
Who's the sender?

SABINE
It's from Lucrèce.

DORANTE
(*After reading the letter.*)
Tell her I'll come.
(*Sabine exits, and Dorante continues.*)
Cliton, rethink your claim
To know which beauty bears that charming name.
Lucrèce is touched now by her devotee,
And from her window wants to talk with me.
If you think it's the other one, your wits are broken.
Why should she write me, when we've never spoken?

CLITON

Sir, on this head I won't debate with you.
Her voice tonight will tell you who is who.

DORANTE

Get into her house by hook or crook, and quiz
Some lackey about how rich her father is.

Scene Eight

Lycas, Dorante

LYCAS
(*Handing Dorante a letter.*)

Sir.

DORANTE

One more letter.
    (*He goes on speaking, after reading it.*)
        I don't know what offense
Has moved my friend Alcippe to truculence,
But tell him to expect me anyway.
I'll come.
    (*Lycas leaves, and Dorante continues to speak.*)
        Last night I got here from Poitiers.
Already, since this morning, I have met
With love, a duel, and a marriage threat.
For a single day, that record's hard to beat.
A lawsuit, and my life would be complete.
I challenge anybody to encumber
Himself with problems worse or more in number,
And wriggle out of them as I can do.
Well, time to face this duel, and see it through.

ACT THREE

Scene One

Philiste, Dorante, Alcippe

PHILISTE

Yes, both of you have managed to behave
Nobly, and neither has been less than brave.
Thank Heaven I was passing by just then
And so could help you to be friends again,
With equal honor and restored good sense.
I'm glad indeed of that coincidence.

DORANTE

I too am glad, especially as I
Have faced a challenge without knowing why.
But now, Alcippe, I beg you to explain
Your rage or rancor, and so relieve my pain.
Has some dark rumor caused your heart to hate?
Speak, and before our friend I'll set you straight.

179

ALCIPPE

Dorante, you know the answer.

DORANTE

                  Try as I will,
I cannot think why you should wish me ill.

ALCIPPE

Well then, to put the matter very clearly,
For two years now I've loved somebody dearly;
She feels the same; we've given vow for vow,
But choose to love in secrecy for now.
Nevertheless, to her I call my own,
Whose favor is reserved for me alone,
You've given a feast, a concert, and a ball.
You well knew how I would resent it all,
For in your vicious plan to put me down
You covered up your presence in the town,
Only emerging from your ambuscade
Today, to boast of the low trick you've played.
Your conduct stuns me, and I plainly see
That all you've done was meant to injure me.

DORANTE

Well, if my courage were still questioned by you,
I'd not seek to correct or pacify you,
And were we rivals, I would draw my blade.
But since I've proven of what stuff I'm made,
Pray listen while I shed a little light.
The lady fair whom I regaled last night
Is a married woman, and so could not be
A proper subject for your jealousy;

                [The Liar]

Some business brought her here not long ago,
And I doubt that she is anyone you know.

ALCIPPE

Dorante, I'm very much relieved. It's splendid
To see our difference so quickly mended.

DORANTE

Another time, Alcippe, don't go along
With mere suspicions, please, however strong.
Don't act until you've found the truth, my friend,
And don't begin with what should be your end.
Farewell.

Scene Two

Philiste, Alcippe

PHILISTE

Still gloomy? Fate is still adverse?

ALCIPPE

I solve one problem, but the next is worse.
Who gave her all those dainties, yesterday eve?
Who was the villain? What can I believe?

PHILISTE

Believe Clarice, who loves you. And understand
That 'twas for someone else that fête was planned.
Your page's error made you rage and burn,
For, fooled himself, he fooled you in your turn.
He and Lucrèce's maids have told me all.
He saw your sweetheart pay Lucrèce a call,
But didn't know that Hippolyte and Daphné
Had happened to be dining there that day.
He saw them leave, with veils upon their faces,
And followed them through town at fifty paces;
The carriage, and the servants' livery
Were certainly Lucrèce's, so that he
Mistook those two for her and your Clarice,
And thus deprived your jealous heart of peace.

[The Liar]

He saw them leave the carriage for a boat
At the water's edge, and once they were afloat
Dishes were served to them, and music played
(Of a rather dreary nature, I'm afraid).
So cheer up now, and yield to my persuasion;
The carriage was but lent for the occasion;
You've been misled; your sweetheart and Lucrèce
Each spent a peaceful night at her address.

ALCIPPE

What dreadful luck I've had, Philiste! I've thus
Inflicted on my love a groundless fuss.

PHILISTE

I'll make your peace with her. But I'm not through yet.
Dorante, too, gave you cause to be upset,
Boasting today of that superb repast
He gave, which was prepared so very fast,
And saying he'd come to town a month ago
And wooed some girl at night incògnito.
In fact, he came from Poitiers yesterday,
Climbed into bed, and slept the night away.

ALCIPPE

But the feast he gave . . .

PHILISTE

    . . . was a lavish lie, it seems.
Or if he gave it, it was in his dreams.

ALCIPPE

Dorante, in the clash of arms that just took place,
Showed too much heart to have a trait so base.

[Act Three / Scene Two]   183

Deceit was never taught in valor's school.
For a man of courage, honesty's the rule.
He'd not dissemble, and he'd rather die
Than practice trickery, or tell a lie.
It can't be so.

Dorante, so I surmise,
Is brave by nature, but from habit lies.
In his case, don't be so incredulous;
Wonder instead at how he hoodwinked us.
Each of us acted like a perfect dupe.
A six-course banquet, starting with the soup!
Four floating concerts, rockets in the air,
All taking just two hours to prepare,
As if that luxury and fine cuisine
Came down from Heaven on some stage machine!
Anyone who believes such evidence,
As you and I did, has more faith than sense.
I saw, though, that his boasting didn't jibe
With the modest treat you'd heard your page describe.
Did you notice that?

ALCIPPE

No, jealousy is blind,
And lets unproven fears possess the mind.
Enough then of Dorante's audacious lies;
I'll seek Clarice now, and apologize.
No wonder that I couldn't make her blush.

PHILISTE

Wait, friend, until tomorrow. There's no rush.
I'll see her first, and pave the way for you.

She'll rage, and I'll appease her when she's through.
You mustn't expose yourself, through eager haste,
To her first burst of fury and distaste.

ALCIPPE

Despite the fading daylight, I can tell
That she's coming this way, with her Isabelle.
As you advise, I'll flee her wrath till she
Can laugh about my fit of jealousy.

Scene Three

Clarice, Isabelle

CLARICE

Come, Isabelle, let's go and join Lucrèce.

ISABELLE

It's still quite early; there's no need to press.
For you, ma'am, she'd do anything under the sun.
I'd hardly asked her, and the note was done.

CLARICE

I'd serve her just as quickly. But tell me, do:
Outside her window, was Géronte in view?
And did you know that the son he thinks so fine
Is the same stranger who gave me such a line?

ISABELLE

We recognized him, both Lucrèce and I,
And when Géronte had told his son goodbye,
Leaving him there alone with his valet,
Sabine brought him the letter right away.
Now you shall speak with him.

CLARICE

                        He's such a fraud!

[*The Liar*]

These days, there's lots of trickery abroad.
Is Dorante the sole young scholar known to fake
A military past, for glamour's sake?
How many talk of Germany, like him,
Telling of battles glorious or grim,
And analyze some setback of our forces
In terms of what it cost in men and horses!
These learn their lore from some gazette, and they
Leave Paris only for some holiday,
Yet here they pose as experts none can doubt
On the great wars they've read or dreamt about.
Dorante, if I am not mistaken, thought
That girls are drawn to he-men who have fought,
And judged that you were likelier to thrill
To a soldier's plume than to a scholar's quill.
To please you, then, he sought to make you see
Not what he is, but what he'd like to be,
Trusting that you would take more kindly to
The new identity he'd forged for you.

CLARICE

In the arts of trickery, he's very deep.
He fooled me first, and then he fooled Alcippe.
That jealous madman tells me, all aquiver,
That I had a fête last night upon the river.
Could anything be farther from the facts?
Alcippe accuses me of faithless acts,
Rants incoherently, and calls me names.
I spent the whole night with Dorante, he claims,
And there was music, it appears, and dance,
And a great banquet, quite the best in France—

So many courses, such fine dishes served
That my poor wits are dizzy and unnerved.

ISABELLE

That Dorante loves, you, ma'am, is what this proves,
And that he's shrewd in gaining what he loves.
He must have known about Alcippe and you,
And made him jealous to estrange you two.
That done, he plays another trick—procures
His father's aid, and has him call on yours.
It took him just one day, the clever devil,
To sway a father and confound a rival.
Your father and his father are at one;
He loves you; you like him; the deal is done.

CLARICE

Done is the word. It's over from the start.

ISABELLE

What, you'd refuse? You've had a change of heart?

CLARICE

You've dropped your guard in dealing with this man.
Explain his further trickery if you can:
He has been married secretly, the swine.
His father's broken off his talks with mine,
Greatly upset, and with a hanging head.

ISABELLE

He's "such a fraud," dear madam, as you said!
He must delight in hoaxing, must adore it,
If he can hoax when there's no reason for it.
The more I think of it, the less I see

[The Liar]

What his intent in bothering you can be.
Whether you ought to talk with him, I doubt.
Are you going to laugh at him, or bawl him out?

CLARICE

I'll tell the man some things he should be told.

ISABELLE

I'd rather leave him standing in the cold.

CLARICE

From curiosity, I'll talk with him.
I glimpse someone, though the light is very dim,
And I might be recognized if it is he;
Let's go to Lucrèce's window, since it's she
In whose name I'll conduct this interview.
My jealous lover, it seems, will have to do:
Once he's recovered from his rage and grief,
I shall fall back on him with great relief.

Scene Four

Dorante, Cliton

DORANTE

It's time, and this is where she bade me be.

CLITON

Her servants gave all sorts of facts to me.
She's the only daughter of a magistrate;
I've told you of her age and her estate.
But, sir, d'you know what I'd find entertaining?
If Lucrèce, like you, were to excel in feigning.
Lord, I'd die laughing if she had the power
To exercise that talent for an hour,
And match you fib for fib, and sometimes hoax
The master hoaxer with her clever jokes.
What stories I would hear from her and you!

DORANTE

The heavens bestow that gift on very few.
It takes alertness, memory, cleverness,
No stammering, and blushing even less.
But come, that window's opening.

Scene Five

Clarice, Isabelle, Lucrèce (at the window);
Dorante, Cliton (below)

CLARICE

(To Isabelle.)
                Isabelle,
While I am talking, be our sentinel.

ISABELLE

Whenever your old man's about to go,
I promise, ma'am, that I shall let you know.
   (Isabelle leaves the window and is no longer seen.)

LUCRÈCE

He's telling Father about you, dear. But come,
Speak out now in my name, and I'll keep mum.

CLARICE

Are you there, Dorante?

DORANTE

              Yes, madam, it is I,
Who in your service wish to live and die.

LUCRÈCE

(*To Clarice.*)

He speaks to you in the same flowery vein.

CLARICE

(*To Lucrèce.*)

It's useless. He should save himself the strain.
Has he recognized my voice already?

CLITON

(*To Dorante.*)

                Sir,
This time I think you're right. It sounds like her.

DORANTE

(*To Clarice.*)

Yes, it is I, who wish I could revoke
The years in which I did not wear your yoke.
Life without seeing you is life misspent,
A lifeless life, a drawn-out discontent,
A death; and I live only, I confess,
When I can be a slave to fair Lucrèce.

CLARICE

(*To Lucrèce.*)

Well, dear, he woos us both in the same fashion.

LUCRÈCE

(*To Clarice.*)

He likes to flaunt his fine talk, and his passion.

        [*The Liar*]

DORANTE

Bound by your laws, I lay my life before you,
Only too glad if I can lose it for you.
Ask what you will, my lady; tell me how
You have resolved that I may serve you now.

CLARICE

There's something I meant to ask, not long ago,
But I shan't ask it, knowing what I know.
You couldn't do it.

DORANTE

Impossible! For you,
There's nothing, nothing that I couldn't do.

CLARICE

Save marry me, since you're already wed.

DORANTE

I, married! You've been wickedly misled.
Whoever said that to you spoke in fun.

CLARICE

(*To Lucrèce.*)
He's an utter rogue.

LUCRÈCE

(*To Clarice.*)
His lies are never done.

[*Act Three / Scene Five*]   193

DORANTE

I've never married, and if this slander will
Affect your feeling—

CLARICE

You'd have me trust you still?

DORANTE

May I be struck by lightning if I lie.

CLARICE

All liars cross their hearts and hope to die.

DORANTE

Lady, if you perceive some good in me
As counterweight to this grave calumny,
Pray let that tip the scales, and entertain
No doubts of what I readily can explain.

CLARICE

(*To Lucrèce.*)
He makes a fib sound honest and naive,
So that one's almost tempted to believe.

DORANTE

To end your doubts, and prove that I speak true,
Let me, tomorrow, give my hand to you.

CLARICE

You'd give your hand to every girl in town.

DORANTE

What you suggest would bring me great renown,
But it might be disapproved of and begrudged.

CLARICE

Well, that's the tone in which you should be judged—
A man who says he's been to war, and yet
Saw action but in dreams or the *Gazette;*
Who, fresh from Poitiers, claims to have been here
Pursuing a belovèd for a year;
Who all night long gives music, feast, and ball,
And yet is snug in bed throughout it all;
Who says he's married, then withdraws the claim.
That's a fine way to build up a good name.
What would you say of such a character?

CLITON

(*To Dorante.*)
Get out of this, and I'll admire you, sir.

DORANTE

(*To Cliton.*)
Don't worry; it will all work out in season.
(*To Clarice.*)
Each of those fictions, madam, was for a reason.
Someday I'll make you see why each was done,
But now I pass to the most important one.
I feigned the marriage (why should I deny
An act for which you'll praise me, by and by?).
I feigned it, and have thus incurred your scorn.
But what if for your sake I was forsworn?

For me?

For you. Unwilling to comply —

(*To Dorante.*)
Please tell me, sir, if you're about to lie.

Wretch! Hold your tongue or I shall tear it out.
(*To Clarice.*)
Since in your service, lady, I am devout,
My love for you forbade me to agree
To a match my father had arranged for me . . .

(*To Lucrèce.*)
Listen. He's off again.

By that finesse
I kept my heart reserved for fair Lucrèce,
And in that marriage, dreamed up on the spot,
Escaped the tying of another knot.
Blame me for stooping to beguile and cheat,
Call me a fraud, a master of deceit,
But praise the strength of my devotion, too,
And call me one whose spirit worships you.
That marriage fends off any other tie;
I flee such bonds; in yours I'd gladly die.

To all but you I am a married man,
And so am free to wed you if I can.

CLARICE

Your newborn passion's all too violent,
And leaves me still unsure of your intent.
How have I gained the favor that you show me,
When you've hardly seen me, sir, and do not know me?

DORANTE

Not know you? Well, your mother's dead (a shame),
And Périandre is your father's name.
He is a judge, sharp-witted and severe.
His income is ten thousand crowns a year.
You lost a brother, fighting in Italy.
You also had a sister named Julie.
Do I know you now? Can you doubt me any more?

CLARICE

He knows *you*, cousin. It's *you* he's aiming for.

LUCRÈCE
(*To herself.*)

God willing!

CLARICE

Let's find out his true intention.
(*To Dorante.*)
Clarice is someone I have meant to mention.
One of your friends believes you fancy her.
How would you like her hand in marriage, sir?

DORANTE

Don't test my heart's sincerity again
By such a question. I've made my feelings plain,
And you know very well how I have parried
Such threats as that by feigning to be married.
It is to you my love and faith are sworn,
While for Clarice I feel contempt and scorn.

CLARICE

I must say that you're downright in your taste.
Clarice is gently born and pleasant-faced,
And, though you see more beauty in Lucrèce,
Could bring a lucky man much happiness.

DORANTE

One great defect, though, spoils her charms for me.

CLARICE

And what is that?

DORANTE

              She's not my cup of tea,
And rather than be married to her, I'd
Go take some Turkish woman for my bride.

CLARICE

Yet in broad daylight, so I understand,
You courted her today, and held her hand.

DORANTE

Someone, I fear, has pulled your leg a bit.

CLARICE

(*To Lucrèce.*)
Listen to him! I bet he'll swear to it.

DORANTE

May Heaven . . .

CLARICE

(*To Lucrèce.*)
I told you!

DORANTE

. . . cleave my tongue in two,
If I spoke to anyone, Lucrèce, but you!

CLARICE

I can't put up with any further lies.
After what I have seen with my own eyes,
You tell me an untruth, and swear it's so,
As if you could deny what we both know.
Goodbye. Be off. It's seldom that I've spent
An evening of such charm and merriment.
Fibbing's a party game I've often played,
And falsehoods are delicious fun to trade.

Scene Six

Cliton, Dorante

CLITON

Ah well, sir; as you see, the truth will out.

DORANTE

I fear, Cliton, that I've been put to rout.

CLITON

I'm sure your plight is better than it looks,
And that you've still a place in her good books.
I'm like that bore of yours whose presence goads
Lovers to speak in secret signs and codes.

DORANTE

Perhaps you're right.

CLITON

　　　　　　Well, that's a big perhaps.

DORANTE

Do you think that I could let my hopes collapse
Because of this rebuff, and lose all heart?

Sir, if you took your high hopes to the mart
And offered them for sale there, my advice
Would be to ask a very modest price.

DORANTE

Why did she not accept my honest passion?

CLITON

Because you lie, sir, in a devilish fashion.

DORANTE

I told the truth.

CLITON

              Yes, but a liar said it,
And coming from your lips it lost all credit.

DORANTE

Then we must see if other lips than mine
Can speak for me, and find her more benign.
I'll go to bed, and hope in dreams to see
Some way to shake her incredulity.
Often the moon controls a woman's mood;
Scorn can conceal a craving to be wooed;
Well, whatsoever she now feels, the night
Will help me ponder till the morning's light.

ACT FOUR

Scene One

Cliton, Dorante

CLITON

D'you think Lucrèce is up and stirring, sir?
It's much too early in the day for her.

DORANTE

Some places are more peopled than they seem,
And in this square I can more sweetly dream.
Seeing her window, I can better raise
Her charming image to my spirit's gaze.

CLITON

Speaking of dreams, sir, did you dream last night
Of some solution to your amorous plight?

DORANTE

I brought to mind a secret that you told
Me yesterday, and said was purest gold:
An open-handed suitor wins the bride.

CLITON

It's a fine secret, but here it's misapplied:
It only works with the flirtatious kind.

DORANTE

Lucrèce, I know, is tasteful and refined,
And any gifts I offered would offend her.
But servants aren't averse to legal tender,
And hers, though she may think they are discreet,
Will gladly talk by way of a receipt.
They'll talk, and often they'll be listened to.
Whatever it costs me, I must buy a few.
If that girl reappears — the one who brought
That note to me — I'm sure she can be bought,
And that without objection she can be
Rewarded for that kind delivery.

CLITON

Well, judging by myself, you're quite correct.
People who love me I do not reject,
And since a present is an act of love,
There's never a gift that I am scornful of.

DORANTE

Many must feel about it as you do.

CLITON

While waiting for Sabine to come in view
And meet with your largesse, let me report
That Alcippe has fought a duel of some sort.

DORANTE

With whom?

[*Act Four / Scene One*]   203

CLITON

Nobody knows; his foe, they say,
Resembled you, sir, in a general way,
And had I ever left your side, I'd guess
That this was more of your outlandishness.

DORANTE

When you went to Lucrèce's house, was I with you then?

CLITON

Oh, sir, can you have fooled me yet again?

DORANTE

We crossed swords yesterday, and I then swore
Never to speak about it anymore,
And yet to you, who know my inmost story
And are my secrets' sole repository,
There's nothing I'm unwilling to disclose.
For some six months, Alcippe and I were foes.
He'd come to Poitiers, and we'd quarreled there,
And though they made us patch up the affair,
We made each other then a secret vow
That we'd resume hostilities somehow.
We met here yesterday and, warmly greeting,
Whispered our challenges and set a meeting.
I shook you off, returned to him, and we
Then took the field of honor privately.
With two deep thrusts I ran him through — a trick
Ensuring that he'll never again be sick.
He fell into a pool of blood.

CLITON

He's dead?

[The Liar]

DORANTE

That's how I left him.

CLITON

Would he had died in bed.
He was a decent man, and there are few . . .

Scene Two

Alcippe, Dorante, Cliton

ALCIPPE

Dear friend, I want to share my joy with you.
Father's here.

DORANTE

Oh?

ALCIPPE

It's the answer to a prayer.

CLITON

(*To Dorante.*)
You do some first-rate dreaming in this square.

DORANTE

Why so much joy? For men like us, it's rather
Strange to be thrilled by visits from one's father.

ALCIPPE

A heart that's overwhelmed by some great good
Thinks that its blurted words are understood.
My news is that the happy day draws nigh

[The Liar]

On which we're to be wed, Clarice and I.
We waited till my sire could be on hand.

DORANTE

Ah, that was what I failed to understand.
I'm glad to hear it. You're off to see Clarice?

ALCIPPE

Yes, I shall share with her the joyous piece
Of news that I have told you on the run.

DORANTE

I thank you all the more for what you've done.
Your love has now no obstacles to fear?

ALCIPPE

While Father's resting from his journey here,
I thought my bride-to-be should know of it.

CLITON
(*To Dorante.*)
The man you killed is looking very fit.

ALCIPPE

I have no doubt that both will acquiesce.
But now, forgive a lover's eagerness.
Farewell.

DORANTE

May Heaven grant you wedded bliss.

Scene Three

Cliton, Dorante

CLITON

Dead, is he? Sir, why hoodwink me like this?
Me, who have access to your heart, and who
Am the sole keeper of your secrets, too!
With such credentials, I thought that I might win
Immunity from being taken in.

DORANTE

What? Do you think that duel was just a fable?

CLITON

Sir, I believe as much as I am able,
But you lie so much, so often, and so widely,
One must be wary, and not trust you idly.
You spare nobody—Christian, Moor, or Jew.

DORANTE

Alcippe's recovery has astonished you.
I left him in a very perilous state,
But recent strides in medicine have been great.
Our fighting men make much use of a cure
Called Sympathetic Powder, and I'm sure
You've heard about the miracles it's done.

CLITON

So far, I've not heard of so much as one,
And I don't believe its virtue is so rare
That a man who's left for dead upon the square
With two big bloody sword holes in his chest
Could in a day be hale and full of zest.

DORANTE

The powder of which you speak's the common kind,
No longer valued. But I've a cure in mind
That brings men back so neatly from death's door
That they forget their pains forevermore.
Who knows it has the wisdom of the ages.

CLITON

Tell me that cure, and you may keep my wages.

DORANTE

I'd gladly give it to you: the secret, though,
Consists of certain Hebrew words I know,
Hard to pronounce and easy to confuse.
They'd be a treasure that you couldn't use.

CLITON

What! You know Hebrew?

DORANTE

             Hebrew? Perfectly.
I speak ten tongues with utmost fluency.

CLITON

You might indeed need ten tongues to supply
The world with such a flow of lie on lie.

You chop up words like mincemeat or pâté.
Inside you there are truths that you might say,
But never a one comes out.

DORANTE

Ah, brainless one!

But Father's here.

Scene Four

Géronte, Dorante, Cliton

GÉRONTE

I've been looking for you, son.

DORANTE

(*Aside.*)
I wasn't seeking *you*, sir. What a bother
To have one's mind distracted by one's father.
And how a father cramps a young man's life!

GÉRONTE

Since you are married now, and have a wife,
I feel I haven't shown a father's heart
If those whom Heaven has joined are still apart.
It makes no sense, and I've a deep, sincere
Wish for your wife to come and join us here.
I'll write to her father — you must do so, too —
And say that, after what I've heard from you,
I'm happy that a girl of high degree,
Charming and chaste, has joined our family.
I'll add that I can't wait till she appears,
Since she's the hope of my declining years,
And that you'll come in person, soon, to bring
Her here to town, for that's the decent thing:
If we merely sent a servant, he'd feel slighted.

DORANTE

By all your courtesies he'd be delighted,
And I'm prepared to go; but he won't allow
His daughter to be brought to Paris now;
She's pregnant.

GÉRONTE

Pregnant!

DORANTE

Yes. Six months along.

GÉRONTE

How deep my joy is at that news! How strong!

DORANTE

You wouldn't have her travel in that state?

GÉRONTE

No, no. My patience, like my joy, is great.
This grandchild is too dear to jeopardize.
Heaven at last has listened to my cries.
When first I see him, I'll perish of delight.
Farewell: I'll change the letter I mean to write,
Sending congratulations and a plea
That he ensure her safe delivery,
Which to my hopeful heart means everything.

DORANTE

(To Cliton.)
Well, off he goes, as happy as a king.

GÉRONTE

(Coming back.)

You too must write him.

DORANTE

Yes, as you said before.
(To Cliton.)

What a dupe!

CLITON

Be still; he's coming back once more.

GÉRONTE

The name of your father-in-law has slipped my mind.
What is it?

DORANTE

No need for trifles of that kind
To give you so much trouble and distress.
When you've sealed the envelope, I'll write the address.

GÉRONTE

All in one hand is better etiquette.

DORANTE

(Aside.)

This is a theme I wish he would forget.
(To Géronte.)

Your hand or mine, it makes no difference.

GÉRONTE

Provincial squires are quick to take offense.

[*Act Four / Scene Four*] 213

DORANTE

Her father knows court customs.

GÉRONTE

All the same,

Tell me —

DORANTE

What?

GÉRONTE

What he's called.

DORANTE

Pyrandre's his name.

GÉRONTE

Pyrandre? 'Twas something else not long ago.
Yes, I recall. 'Twas Armédon, I know.

DORANTE

Yes, that's his name; the other is his estate.
He used the latter in the wars. Of late,
He's known by either name, and if and when
He isn't Armédon, he's Pyrandre then.

GÉRONTE

It's a vanity that custom does not blame.
Back in my younger years, I did the same.
Farewell, I'll write to him.

[The Liar]

Scene Five

Dorante, Cliton

DORANTE

Well, I saved my hide.

CLITON

You need a perfect memory, when you've lied.

DORANTE

My loss of memory was redeemed by wit.

CLITON

Your fabrications soon will come unknit.
After that crucial blunder that you made,
Exposure of the rest can't be delayed.
Lucrèce's household know how you're forsworn;
So does Clarice, who so resents your scorn
That at the first occasion she will aim
To cover you with disrepute and shame.

DORANTE

Your fear's well grounded, and I see that I'd
Best hurry and get Lucrèce upon my side.
Well, here's an opportune and welcome sight.

Scene Six

Dorante, Sabine, Cliton

DORANTE

Dear friend, I was beside myself last night,
And once I'd read that letter I was too
Enraptured to give proper thanks to you.
But now I'll make it up to you, if I may.

SABINE

You mustn't think, sir —

DORANTE

Here.

SABINE

It's not my way
To look for —

DORANTE

Please.

SABINE

No, no.

DORANTE

Come, take it, now.
I like to show my gratitude somehow.
Hold out your hand.

CLITON

What a fuss the girl does make!
I'll counsel her a bit, for pity's sake.
These quaint refusals, dear, in such a case
As this, are altogether out of place.
In your profession one must not be loath
To take with one hand, or to grab with both.
Confess that, in delivering a letter,
You hope for something, and the more the better.
If rain were money, sweetheart, you can bet
I'd stand out in it and get soaking wet.
This is an age when each man's for himself;
Great souls no longer show disdain for pelf.
Follow my teachings, now; be smart and thrifty.
Shall we be partners, and go fifty-fifty?

SABINE

You ask too much.

DORANTE

(*To Sabine.*)
In time, it's my intention
To do for you some things I shan't now mention.
But since 'twas you that note was carried by,
Would you consent to take her my reply?

[*Act Four* / *Scene Six*]   217

Gladly, although I cannot promise, sir,
That it will be received or read by her.
I'll do my best.

CLITON

(*To Dorante.*)
You see, you've won her love;
She's sweet as a bride and supple as a glove.

DORANTE

(*To Cliton.*)
Your secret works.
(*To Sabine.*)
Well, take it anyway.
She's not averse to me, I hope and pray.
I'll come back soon to learn of her reaction.

SABINE

I'll try to serve you to your satisfaction.

Scene Seven

Cliton, Sabine

CLITON

Some actions, as you see, speak louder than words.
This man strews coin as if to feed the birds.
I, at his side, can be of use to you.

SABINE

Let the coins rain down, and I'll know what to do.

CLITON

You're catching on.

SABINE

                    With my demure "no, no"s,
I'm not so innocent as you suppose.
I know my business, friend, and I succeed
As well by daintiness as you by greed.

CLITON

Since you know your business, is my master's suit
Likely, in your opinion, to bear fruit?
Is she warm toward him? Or is she cold and steely?

SABINE

Since he's so kind a man, I'll tell you freely.
His ardor has impressed her, and Lucrèce is
Anything but unmoved by his addresses.
The whole night long, she didn't sleep a wink,
And she is half in love with him, I think.

CLITON

How dare she then be so contemptuous of
This man with whom, you say, she's half in love?
Last night, she gave him only sneers and scorn.
He's a catch, my dear — both handsome and well born.
This halfway love is all too harsh, and he
Ought to forget Lucrèce, it seems to me.

SABINE

Don't let him act in haste. She loves him, truly.

CLITON

If so, her words don't pamper him unduly.
I try to understand her, but I fail.

SABINE

As they say, she has a tiger by the tail.
She loves him, yet she's greatly troubled by
Discovering that his custom is to lie.
Just yesterday, in the Tuileries, she heard
Him talk at length without one honest word;
Since when, repeatedly, he's lied again.

CLITON

The greatest liar is truthful now and then.

[*The Liar*]

SABINE

She has good reason to mistrust and doubt him.

CLITON

She ought to feel more confidence about him.
He was awake all night, tossing and sighing.

SABINE

By any chance have you, too, taken to lying?

CLITON

Certainly not, dear. I'm a man of honor.

SABINE

What of Clarice? Has he ceased to dote upon her?

CLITON

He feels no love for her . . .

SABINE

No?

CLITON

Only disdain.

SABINE

He needn't fear, then, that he sighs in vain.
When Lucrèce observed, just now, that he was about,
She quickly gave me orders to go out,
In case he wished to send some word to her.
If he loves her truly, I think she won't demur.

[Act Four / Scene Seven]

Be off; don't tell me what to do, my dear.
Trust me to tell her what she ought to hear.

CLITON

Farewell. If you will just apply my training,
I promise you that coins will soon be raining.

Scene Eight

Sabine, Lucrèce

SABINE

Ah, what a happy girl I soon shall see!
But here she comes. How eager she must be!
Her eyes are sharp; she saw this billet-doux.

LUCRÈCE

Well, what did he and his valet say to you?

SABINE

Master and man were perfectly agreed.
The master loves you, and here's some prose to read.

LUCRÈCE
(*After reading it.*)
Dorante pretends he's full of amorous heat,
But I have seen enough of his deceit;
I doubt his words, and shall not be deceived.

SABINE

I doubt them too, but his coin must be believed.

LUCRÈCE

He's given you something?

SABINE

Look.

LUCRÈCE

And you took his gift?

SABINE

Madam, to give your troubled heart a lift
And make you surer of his heartfelt sighs,
I took these coins. Such witness never lies.
I'll let the world decide if someone who
Rewards your maid is not in love with you;
What else could such a noble gesture mean?

LUCRÈCE

I don't object to your good luck, Sabine,
But you shouldn't have accepted it, and so
Another time you mustn't let me know.

SABINE

But — to this generous man — what shall be said?

LUCRÈCE

Tell him I tore his letter up unread.

SABINE

Ah, my good luck, how quickly you are flown!

LUCRÈCE

Add, if you like, some kind words of your own.
Tell him how changeable is womankind,
And how, in time, a girl can change her mind.
And tell him at what times and places he,

[*The Liar*]

As if by accident, might encounter me.
He's such a trickster that I must go slow.

SABINE

If you knew what pains he's said to undergo,
You'd doubt no longer that his love is strong.
He sighs and groans and tosses, all night long.

LUCRÈCE

To moderate the pains of which you tell,
Give him some hope, but lots of fear as well;
Shuttle him twixt the two, but don't commit
My heart, or lead him to despair of it.

Scene Nine

CLARICE

Well, it's you he's after, and I'm rid of him.
The loss, to me, is anything but grim.
Alcippe's my compensation. His father's here.

LUCRÈCE

So the end of your uncertainties is near?

CLARICE

The end is near for me, and you're all set
To make a curious conquest. Don't forget
The fibs he told me.

LUCRÈCE

                    He lied then, but somehow
I'm certain that he's being truthful now.

CLARICE

Perchance he is, but that's a big perchance.

LUCRÈCE

We know Dorante's a liar, the best in France,
But if he courts me faithfully, it may be
That he'll come to seem an honest man to me.

CLARICE

If, knowing his great fault, you still can love him,
Do play your cards well, and be wary of him.

LUCRÈCE

I only meant, just now, that I'm inclined
To trust him; I did not have love in mind.

CLARICE

From trust to love is but the briefest span.
Believe his love and you'll soon admire the man.
Those two things go together, as soon we learn:
Think that you're loved, and soon you'll love in turn.

LUCRÈCE

What seems an amorous state of mind can be
No more, at times, than curiosity.

CLARICE

I'll try to think so, if you wish me to.

SABINE

You make me very angry, both of you.
What is the point of all this high-flown chat?
Stop sounding coy, and running on like that.
You'll only miss the boat, as people say.

LUCRÈCE

Ignore this crazy woman; and, by the way,
When we first met him yesterday, and he
Addressed you with such fervent gallantry,
I think you listened with an eager ear.
Was it love or curiosity, my dear?

CLARICE

Pure curiosity, and the intent
To chuckle at each silly compliment.

LUCRÈCE

The note he sent I dealt with in that fashion.
I took it, read it, but not with any passion.
Pure curiosity, and the intent
To chuckle at the flowery prose he'd sent.

CLARICE

Reading and listening aren't the same to me:
One's a great favor, one's a mere courtesy.
But if your hopes work out, I shall rejoice.
I'll feel no envy, since I've made my choice.

LUCRÈCE

Sabine will tell him I've torn up his letter.

CLARICE

But reading it, as you did, has pleased you better.
You're curious, after all.

LUCRÈCE

Like you, my lass.

CLARICE

So be it; but now it's time we went to Mass.

LUCRÈCE

(*To Clarice.*)

Let's go.

(To Sabine.)
If you see him, you know what to say.

SABINE

I do, ma'am; I was not born yesterday.
I know what ails the two of you, and I'm sure
That it's an ailment I know how to cure.
This is a man to gather while you may.

LUCRÈCE

No doubt.

SABINE

(Looking at the coin in her hand.)
Now I'll put this piece of rain away.

ACT FIVE

Scene One

Géronte, Philiste

GÉRONTE

It's lucky I ran into you, for I
Have certain questions you can satisfy.
You, like my son, read law once in Poitiers,
And got to know its people, I daresay.
Thus you can readily give me information
About Pyrandre's background, wealth, and station.

PHILISTE

Who's this Pyrandre?

GÉRONTE

He's a citizen who
Is noble, I gather, though not well-to-do.

PHILISTE

In all Poitiers there's nobody at all
Who bears that name — or none that I recall.

GÉRONTE

Perhaps you'll find his other name less strange;
He sometimes uses Armédon for a change.

PHILISTE

Still stranger.

GÉRONTE

He's the father of Orphise,
On whose great beauty everyone agrees.
You surely know the name of that fair creature,
Who is this region's most enchanting feature?

PHILISTE

Orphise, Pyrandre, Armédon, all three,
Are quite unknown to Poitiers and to me.
If you would like some further evidence —

GÉRONTE

You're feigning ignorance in my son's defense,
But I know how he loves Orphise, with whom,
After some trysting visits to her room,
He was discovered there, alone with her;
And how his pistol caused a dreadful stir,
Forcing them to be married then and there.

[Act Five / Scene One]   231

I know it all, and I give the happy pair
A father's blessing. There's no reason for
His friends to keep his secret any more.

PHILISTE

Dorante's been wed in secret? Is that the truth?

GÉRONTE

I am indulgent, and forgive his youth.

PHILISTE

Who told you?

GÉRONTE

He himself.

PHILISTE

                    Since he's your source,
He can inform you better than I, of course,
And answer all your enquiries about it.
It's quite a story. I don't mean you should doubt it,
But he has an inventive streak, it seems,
And I can't vouch for other people's dreams.

GÉRONTE

Are you implying that his tale's untrue?

PHILISTE

No, no. His word is good. Believe him, do.
But yesterday he served us a collation
Concocted out of pure imagination,
And if this marriage tale is like it, you'll
Find out that it's the sheerest cock-and-bull.

[*The Liar*]

GÉRONTE

Do you take pleasure in provoking me?

PHILISTE

Good heavens, you're as gullible as we.
If you never have — forgive my frankness, please —
Another daughter-in-law than this Orphise,
Your near relations will be blithe and gay.
You understand. Farewell, I've said my say.

[*Act Five* / *Scene One*]

Scene Two

Géronte

GÉRONTE

O brazen youth! O foolish age! Misled,
I've brought disgrace upon my own gray head!
What father has a better cause to grieve?
What worse blow could a generous heart receive?
Dorante's a trickster who, as now I learn,
Deceiving me, makes me deceive in turn;
He spins a lie, which then he spreads abroad
By making me the herald of a fraud.
As if it weren't enough that I must pass
My days in blushing for his sins, alas,
The rogue exploits my trust, and causes me
To blush as well for my credulity.

Scene Three

Géronte, Dorante, Cliton

GÉRONTE

Are you a gentleman?

DORANTE

(*Aside.*)
Ah me, what a bother!
(*To Géronte.*)
There's little question, sir, since you're my father.

GÉRONTE

You think it is enough to be my son?

DORANTE

All France would say the same, in unison.

GÉRONTE

Aren't you aware, as every Frenchman knows,
From what that honored title first arose?
Virtue alone once earned that dignity
For those whose blood has passed it down to me.

DORANTE

I know, sir, that high rank, since Noah's flood,
Was gained by virtue and passed down by blood.

[*Act Five / Scene Three*]   235

GÉRONTE

The humblest blood, through virtue's aid, can climb;
The noblest blood can sink through vice and crime.
One inclination is the other's curse;
All that one does, the other can reverse,
And in your base dishonesty you are not
The gentleman I thought I had begot.

DORANTE

I?

GÉRONTE

   Hear me, you whose falsehoods are a breach
Of honor, and degrade the gift of speech.
A would-be gentleman, who lies so much,
Forgoes that title, and was never such.
Is there a blacker stain, an action more
Debased in one brought up to shine in war?
Is there a vice, a failing, that is worse—
To which a noble heart is more averse?
When such a man has lied, his only way
To expunge it is to rush into the fray,
Hoping that blood will wash away somehow
The mark that shame has stamped upon his brow.

DORANTE

Who tells you that I lie, sir?

GÉRONTE

           Who? For shame!
See if you can remember your wife's name
In the tale you told me, and which I have spread.

         [The Liar]

CLITON

(*To Dorante.*)

Say you forgot it while asleep in bed.

GÉRONTE

And see if you can brazenly relate
The name of your father-in-law, and his estate.
Come, dazzle me with fresh inventions, too.

CLITON

(*To Dorante.*)

If you can't remember, wit will have to do.

GÉRONTE

With what embarrassment must I confess
That I was hoodwinked by your brazenness;
That a man of my age could believe the lies
A shameless man of your age dared devise!
You've made of me a butt, a laughingstock,
A feeble-minded oaf whom all may mock.
Come: did I hold a dagger at your heart?
What rage or violence was there on my part?
If Clarice did not appeal to you, what need
Was there for such a low, dishonest deed?
Did you not know that I would take no action
That did not seek your joy and satisfaction —
I, whose extreme indulgence has been shown
In sanctioning your choice of an unknown?
The boundless love I've given you has won
No answer from your heart. Ungrateful son,
You've paid me back with sham and fakery,
And have no love, respect, or fear for me.
Go, I disown you.

DORANTE

Listen, Father, please.

GÉRONTE

To what? To your impromptu fantasies?

DORANTE

No, the plain truth, sir.

GÉRONTE

Do you tell it, ever?

CLITON

(*To Dorante.*)
He just can't see that telling lies is clever.

DORANTE

I'm charmed by a beauty whom I'd scarcely seen
When she became my goddess and my queen.
I mean Lucrèce, whom I believe you know.

GÉRONTE

I know her and her family, that's so.
Her father is my friend.

DORANTE

Thus overcome
By charms to which my soul could but succumb,
I found your choosing of Clarice to be,
Though kindly meant, a source of agony.
But as I didn't know then if Lucrèce
Could pass your test for fortune and noblesse,

I dared not yet inform you of the name
Of her whose glance had set my heart aflame.
Nor had I reckoned, sir, until this time,
That wit, in love's defense, could be a crime.
But if I dared to ask a favor, sir,
Knowing now what high rank belongs to her,
I would entreat you by the deep and true
Bonds of affection joining me to you
To help me claim this girl for mine alone;
Pray ask her sire's consent; I'll seek her own.

GÉRONTE

You're still deceiving me.

DORANTE

If you don't trust mè,
Then trust Cliton, the soul of honesty.
He knows my secrets.

GÉRONTE

You should be disgusted
That, of you two, it's he who can be trusted—
That even your father, doubting what you say,
Listens more trustingly to your valet.
But hear me: I'll relent, regardless of
My rage, and once more show a father's love.
Once more, for your sake, I shall risk my honor.
I know Lucrèce and I shall call upon her,
But if you change your mind, if you dare make—

DORANTE

I'll go with you, for reassurance' sake.

Stay here, stay here, and do not dare to follow.
I'm full of doubt, and fear your words are hollow.
But rest assured that if you play Lucrèce
Some wretched trick or hoax or sly finesse,
You'd better flee my sight, or be aware
Of the great vengeful oath that now I swear:
I swear by all the lights of heaven that shine
That you'll not die save by this hand of mine,
And that your worthless blood shall be the cost
Of compensating me for honor lost.

Scene Four

Dorante, Cliton

DORANTE

I'm not at all afraid of such a threat.

CLITON

You sound defiant, sir; don't give in yet.
That clever wit of yours, that's fooled him twice,
Should boldly strike again. That's my advice.
The third time, as they say, is make or break.

DORANTE

Don't tease me now, Cliton, for Heaven's sake.
I've a new worry like an aching tooth.

CLITON

Is it remorse for having told the truth?
Or are you plotting some new trickiness?
Right now I wonder if you love Lucrèce,
For you're so full of twists and turns of wit
That, when you speak, I hear the opposite.

DORANTE

I love her: that's one thing you needn't doubt.
It's what might happen that I fret about.

If the fathers don't agree, my hope's cut short
And the ship of my desire is sunk in port.
On the other hand, if they see eye to eye,
How certain of the daughter's love am I?
I glimpsed that beauty on the street today.
Her friend is most attractive, I must say.
Now that I've studied her, though not mistaken
In my first love, I feel a little shaken.
My heart's divided now betwixt the pair,
And could be hers, were I not pledged elsewhere.

CLITON

Why then did you display such passion, and
Entreat your sire to ask Lucrèce's hand?

DORANTE

He wouldn't have believed me otherwise.

CLITON

Even your truths, sir, are a lot like lies.

DORANTE

'Twas the only way I could appease his ire.
I curse whoever undeceived my sire.
With that fictitious marriage, I was free
To take my time and choose advisedly.

CLITON

But Lucrèce's friend is, after all, Clarice.

DORANTE

Yes, yes, that's so, and my heart should be at peace.
Lucky Alcippe! Just now, that slipped my mind.

Well, he has only got what I declined.
My choice is made. No more uncertainties.

CLITON

You've brushed her off as if she were Orphise.

DORANTE

I'll take back to Lucrèce my wandering soul,
Which for a time the other all but stole.
But here's Sabine.

Scene Five

Dorante, Sabine, Cliton

DORANTE

What of my letter, friend?
Did those fair hands receive what I had penned?

SABINE

Yes, sir, but —

DORANTE

But?

SABINE

She tore it up, alas.

DORANTE

Unread?

SABINE

Unread.

DORANTE

And did you let that pass?

[*The Liar*]

SABINE

I didn't. But what a talking-to she gave me!
I fear that she'll dismiss me. Heaven save me.

DORANTE

She'll soon calm down; but let this ease your pain.
Hold out your hand.

SABINE

Oh!

DORANTE

Speak to her once again;
I shan't give in so quickly to despair.

CLITON

Look at that sweet thing with her dainty air.
Your coin made all her troubles disappear.
She'll tell you more now than you want to hear.

DORANTE

She tore my letter up unread, you say?

SABINE

That's what she said to tell you, anyway;
But truly—

CLITON

She knows her trade, I'm telling you.

SABINE

She didn't tear it up; she read it through.
I can't mislead so generous a man.

CLITON

Name me a smarter baggage if you can.

DORANTE

She doesn't hate me, it appears?

SABINE

Why, no.

DORANTE

Does she love me?

SABINE

No again.

DORANTE

You're sure?

SABINE

Just so.

DORANTE

Is there someone else?

SABINE

Not one.

DORANTE

Will my suit go well?

I don't know.

DORANTE

Come now, tell me.

SABINE

What shall I tell?

DORANTE

The truth.

SABINE

I've told it.

DORANTE

Could I be loved by her?

SABINE

Perhaps.

DORANTE

But when?

SABINE

When she can trust you, sir.

DORANTE

When she can trust me! What joy those words impart!

SABINE

When she trusts you, you can say you've won her heart.

DORANTE

Then I can say so now, and boast about it;
I've pledged my word to her; she cannot doubt it.
My father —

SABINE

Well, here they come, Clarice and she.

Scene Six

Clarice, Dorante, Lucrèce, Sabine, Cliton

CLARICE

(*To Lucrèce.*)
Be careful. Truth is not his specialty.
You know this weakness; best avoid all haste.

DORANTE

(*To Clarice.*)
Oh, beauty on whom all my hopes are based—

CLARICE

(*To Lucrèce.*)
I thought he scorned me, but he looks my way.

LUCRÈCE

(*To Clarice.*)
His glances may by chance have gone astray.
Let's see if he persists.

DORANTE

(*To Clarice.*)
                  When you're afar,
How dull and dead the passing minutes are!
How well I know now that an hour apart
Can be sheer torture for a lover's heart!

[*Act Five / Scene Six*]

CLARICE

(*To Lucrèce.*)

Same story.

LUCRÈCE

(*To Clarice.*)

But look at what he wrote me, do.

CLARICE

(*To Lucrèce.*)

Ssh. Listen.

LUCRÈCE

You think his words are meant for you!

CLARICE

(*To Lucrèce.*)

Let's clear this up. Dorante, does this mean you love me?

DORANTE

(*To Clarice.*)

Alas, your proud heart takes no notice òf me!
Since in your eyes I found what I was seeking—

CLARICE

(*To Lucrèce.*)

Do you still think it's you to whom he's speaking?

LUCRÈCE

(*To Clarice.*)

I'm stunned.

CLARICE

(*To Lucrèce.*)
Let's see how far this hoax will go.

LUCRÈCE

(*To Clarice.*)
It's a clumsy joke, considering what we know.

CLARICE

(*To Lucrèce.*)
See how the man divides his love between us;
By night you're Aphrodite; by day I'm Venus.

DORANTE

(*To Clarice.*)
Ah, you're conferring. Whatever she may say,
Listen to kinder counselors, I pray.
In her advice I fear there's no goodwill.
I've given her some cause to wish me ill.

LUCRÈCE

(*To herself.*)
Indeed you have, and when I take revenge—

CLARICE

(*To Dorante.*)
What she was telling me is very strange.

DORANTE

Some jealous fantasy. 'Twould not surprise me.

CLARICE

No doubt. But tell me, do you recognize me?

[*Act Five / Scene Six*]   251

DORANTE

Do I recognize you? What a curious joke!
Just yesterday, in the Tuileries, we spoke.
And you became my queen and conqueress.

CLARICE

But if I trust her story nonetheless,
There's someone else already whom you adore—

DORANTE

What? Someone else whom I've betrayed you for?
Oh, rather I were flayed, and hanged, and buried!

CLARICE

What's more, if she can be believed, you're married.

DORANTE

Madam, I think you're toying with me when
You prompt me to explain to you again
How, hoping to be yours alone for life,
I tell all others that I have a wife.

CLARICE

And yet before you'd offer me your hand
You'd take a Turkish bride, I understand.

DORANTE

Before I wed another, I'd marry you
In the Atlas Mountains, if you wished me to.

CLARICE

But do you not regard Clarice with scorn?

DORANTE

It was for you that all my schemes were born,
And there's no trick I wouldn't play to win you.

CLARICE

I'm stunned now in my turn, and can't continue.
Listen, Lucrèce—

DORANTE

(*To Cliton.*)
"Lucrèce," she said, I swear!

CLITON

Touché! Lucrèce is the prettier of the pair,
And I'm the one who guessed which one was which.
If we'd had a bet upon it, I'd be rich.

DORANTE

(*To Cliton.*)
The voice I heard last night was hers, I claim.

CLITON

(*To Dorante.*)
Clarice was speaking in Lucrèce's name,
And from her window. I learned that from Sabine.

DORANTE

Ah . . . Well, the other, also, is a queen,
And since, just now, I found her beauty striking,
My error is already to my liking.
Don't give me away, Cliton, and you shall see
Me use, for this new love, new strategy:
My style won't change, but I shall change my goal.

[*Act Five / Scene Six*]   253

LUCRÈCE

(*To Clarice.*)

Now we shall see how brazen is his soul.
He ought to find your questions staggering.

CLARICE

(*To Dorante.*)

Since she's my friend, she's told me everything.
Last night you loved her, and felt scorn for me.
To which of us did you speak dishonestly?
Your words to her were passionate, if true.

DORANTE

What? Since my return I've spoken but to you.

CLARICE

Were you not speaking with Lucrèce last night?

DORANTE

Did you not try on me a clever sleight,
And didn't I recognize your voice with ease?

CLARICE

Is he going to tell the truth now, if you please?

DORANTE

To pay you back, I had the wit and sense
To let you keep on with that crude pretense;
I let you pass for her you feigned to be,
And thus I fooled you more than you fooled me.
Don't think that I was taken in. Come, come:
When next you choose a dupe, pick one that's dumb.

You sought to trick me; I in turn tricked *you*,
Though with a touch of scorn that wasn't true,
For truly I adore you, and regret
The empty days and years before we met.

CLARICE

If you love me, why pretend that you are wed
When your father comes to see me in your stead?
How did that falsehood shape things for the better?

LUCRÈCE

(*To Dorante.*)
If you love *her*, why write me such a letter?

DORANTE

(*To Lucrèce.*)
I prize your anger and its hidden source;
If you're angry, you must care for me, of course.
But now, enough of tricks and cleverness.
The truth is, I love no one but Lucrèce.

CLARICE

(*To Lucrèce.*)
What a gross deceiver! Must you hear him out?

DORANTE

(*To Lucrèce.*)
Once you have heard me, you'll be free of doubt.
Last night, you lent your name — and window — to
Clarice, who played a trick that I saw through;
Since you abetted her in deviousness,
I've taken a small revenge on you, Lucrèce.

LUCRÈCE

But in the Tuileries, I heard you say—

DORANTE

I flirted with Clarice there yesterday—

CLARICE

(*To Lucrèce.*)
What rot. How long do you propose to hear it?

DORANTE

(*To Lucrèce.*)
She had my flattering words, but you my spirit,
In which I hid the flame your eyes had lit
Until my father should approve of it.
Since all I said was pure imagination,
You still know nothing of my rank and station.

CLARICE

(*To Lucrèce.*)
He piles up fraud on fraud before our eyes;
It's all but sleight-of-hand and cunning lies.

DORANTE

(*To Lucrèce.*)
It's you alone my dazzled heart could love.

LUCRÈCE

(*To Dorante.*)
That's not what your behavior seems to prove.

DORANTE

If my father's now beneath your father's roof
Conferring, is that not sufficient proof?

LUCRÈCE

That's telling evidence. I'll rack my brain
And see what other grounds for doubt remain.

DORANTE

(To Lucrèce.)
May all your groundless worries disappear.
(To Clarice.)
Clarice dear, love Alcippe for many a year.
Without my marriage in Poitiers, he'd never
Have claimed you, but I shall not tell him ever.
'Twill be a secret between me and you.
But here he comes, and I see my father too.

Scene Seven

Alcippe, Géronte, Dorante,
Clarice, Lucrèce, Sabine, Cliton, Isabelle

ALCIPPE

(*Coming out of Clarice's house, and addressing her.*)
Our sires agree; our wedding can be planned!

GÉRONTE

(*Coming out of Lucrèce's house, and addressing her.*)
Your father bids Dorante to ask your hand.

ALCIPPE

(*To Clarice.*)
One word from you, and the knot's as good as tied.

GÉRONTE

(*To Lucrèce.*)
One word from you, and you shall be his bride.

DORANTE

(*To Lucrèce.*)
Don't balk my heart's desires, I pray you. Come.

ALCIPPE

What's this? Have both of you been stricken dumb?

[*The Liar*]

CLARICE

In all things, let my father have his way.

LUCRÈCE

It is a daughter's duty to obey.

GÉRONTE

(To Lucrèce.)
Come then, my dear, and be obedient.

ALCIPPE

(To Clarice.)
Come then, my dear, and give your sweet consent.
(Alcippe goes back into Clarice's house with her and
Isabelle, and the others go into Lucrèce's house.)

SABINE

(To Dorante, as he enters the house.)
Once you are married, it won't rain at all.

DORANTE

For you, I'll change it to a waterfall.

SABINE

You won't remember. Your gratitude won't last.
My skills are worthless when the need is past.

CLITON

(Alone.)
When his own tricks get a trickster in a scrape,
He may not find it easy to escape,
But you who feared his fate might go awry
Should learn from our young hero how to lie.

[Act Five / Scene Seven]

259